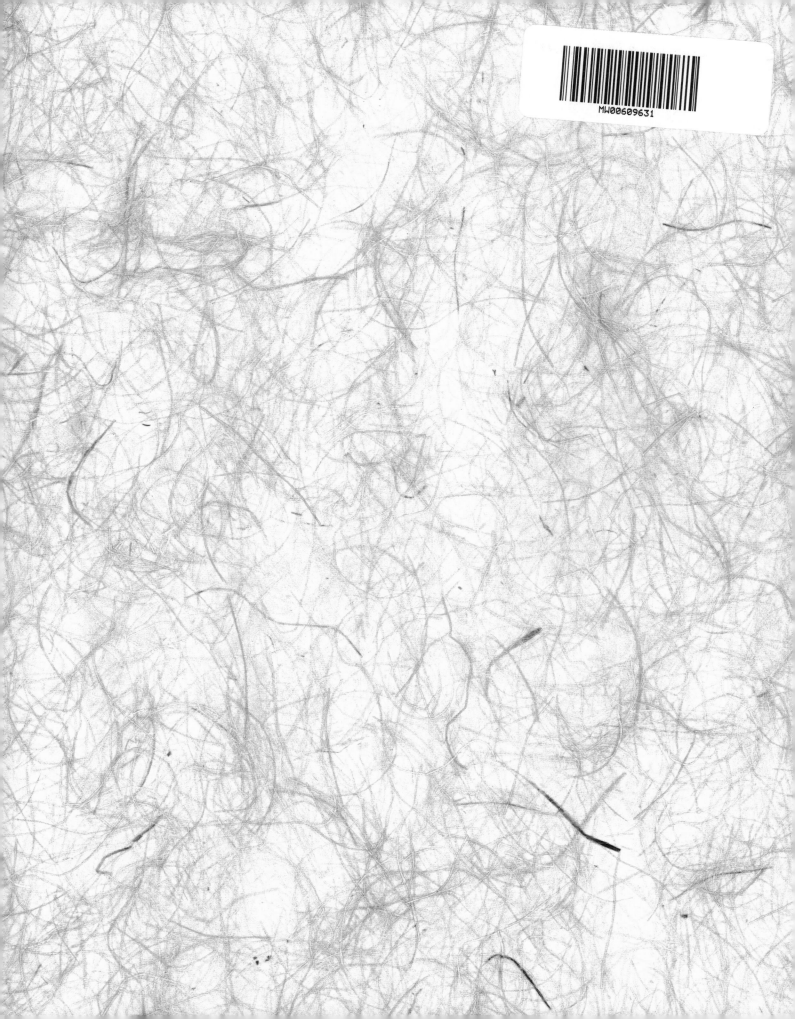

Early Fenton Rarities
1907-1938

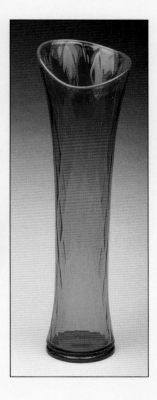

Thomas K. Smith

Schiffer Publishing Ltd

4880 Lower Valley Road, Atglen, PA 19310 USA

Dedications

This book is dedicated to the entire Fenton family, but especially Wilmer C. (Bill) and Don Fenton. Everyone who knew them loved them and misses them. I was privileged to be close friends with both of them. Neither one of them ever knew a stranger. Each of us has our special memories and stories of Bill and Don. Celebrate their lives and pass on your memories to future generations of collectors.

Special Dedication goes to: Mr.'s. Frank L. Fenton and Frank M. Fenton. What more can you say about these gentleman that has not already been said? They were and are icons of the American glass making industry. Frank L. developed many of the beautiful designs in this book. Frank M. and his brother, Bill, continued the tradition of excellence over the second fifty years. The year 2005 will mark the company's 100th anniversary. That speaks volumes.

Library of Congress Cataloging-in-Publication Data

Smith, Thomas K.
  Early Fenton rarities, 1907-1938 / by Thomas K. Smith.
     p. cm.
  ISBN 0-7643-2287-7 (hardcover)
1. Fenton Art Glass Company—Catalogs. 2. Glassware—West Virginia—Williamstown—History—20th century—Catalogs. 3. Glass, Colored—West Virginia—Williamstown—Catalogs. 4. Glassware—Collectors and collecting—United States—Catalogs. I. Title.

NK5198.F4A4 2005
748.2'09754'22—dc22
                                                2005002315

Designed by Mark David Bowyer
Type set in Zapf Chancery Bd BT/Souvenir Lt BT

ISBN: 0-7643-2287-7
Printed in China
1 2 3 4

Published by Schiffer Publishing Ltd.
4880 Lower Valley Road
Atglen, PA 19310
Phone: (610) 593-1777; Fax: (610) 593-2002
E-mail: Info@schifferbooks.com

For the largest selection of fine reference books on this and related subjects, please visit our web site at
www.schifferbooks.com
We are always looking for people to write books on new and related subjects. If you have an idea for a book please contact us at the above address.

This book may be purchased from the publisher.
Include $3.95 for shipping.
Please try your bookstore first.
You may write for a free catalog.

In Europe, Schiffer books are distributed by
Bushwood Books
6 Marksbury Ave.
Kew Gardens
Surrey TW9 4JF England
Phone: 44 (0) 20 8392-8585; Fax: 44 (0) 20 8392-9876
E-mail: info@bushwoodbooks.co.uk
Free postage in the U.K., Europe; air mail at cost.

Contents

Acknowledgments

My first thanks and love go to my parents, Keith and Marilyn Smith. I know at times I gave them some early gray hairs and they were not sure at first about this glass thing. I am so fortunate to have them and even more fortunate that they are still here. I hope this book makes them proud.

My love, thanks, and apologies to my girlfriend, Cheryl Shorr. Not only does she endure my show schedule, but she has also been widowed many weekends this past year due to the traveling and time spent working on the book. Hopefully she will get her full-time boyfriend back now.

There are many more people to acknowledge, and they appear in no particular order of importance.

Carolyn and Woody Kriner, New York: Woody was the first person I met when I got out of my car at the Knight's Inn. It was my first convention in 1988 and I did not know a soul. I met my Fenton mentor, Carolyn, a few minutes later. They, along with the group from the Western New York Club, took me under their wings, showed me the ropes, and treated me like family. They are two of my most treasured friends. Allow me a personal and private tribute to the New York gang. "Bulk."

John Walk: John has become one of my best friends in the last ten years. He is a friend in the true sense of the word. I admire his passion for Fenton Glass. His mother, Bonnie, always treats me like family, as did his late father, John. Everyone should be so lucky to have such friends.

Mr. Frank M. Fenton: It is an honor to be considered his friend. We are all so fortunate that he has graciously shared his knowledge and his love of glass for the last thirty years. He is always generous with his time and expertise. He is a treasure. "Thank you, Frank." This book is for you.

I also wish to thank the entire Fenton Family: George, Nancy, Tom, Mike, Shelley, Randy, Christine, Scott, Lynn, and others. They are a family in the true sense of the word. It is a privilege to have known all of them these past eighteen years. As many of you know, the family has had some very personal losses the last few years. Elinor, her husband, Bill, and son, Don, passed away, but their memories will always be with us. Elinor was always so gracious, Bill always had a funny story or joke, and Don always made you feel like how you and your family were the most important. I miss them and think about them every day. As long as we keep their memories alive and share them with others, theirs will be a wonderful legacy.

Jennifer Maston, caretaker of the Fenton Museum: Jennifer is a great friend and is always helpful with any questions I have. She was also helpful in scheduling photography at the museum. What a great job she has. She works with Frank Fenton every day.

I must also give a big thanks to Jeff Kelly, Warehouse Supervisor at the Fenton Art Glass Company. During the two days photographing pieces at the Fenton Museum, Jeff made himself readily available to open and close cases so that I could have timely access to the glass.

Pam Dick: Pam is tireless in her research and museum cataloging. She has done many seminars for collectors' clubs. Pam made sure I had access to any of the glass I needed to photograph. She's great.

Dr. James Measell, assistant historian at the Fenton Art Glass Company: Dr. Measell is always there to identify the glass anyone brings in. His contributions to glass research and books have been invaluable. It will be a pleasure to work with him for many years to come.

Mary Catherine Smith: My former wife, she was invaluable as she typed and filed all the text and the captions. If I had to hunt and peck all those letters, this book would not have been written. She is a wonderful person and we have remained good friends.

Millie Coty: She has been one of John Walk's any my best friends and colleagues for more than fifteen years. She has been invaluable in editing and improving the quality of our books. She has been involved in the national Fenton clubs for many years and has a great knowledge of all antiques.

One gentleman I must mention is the late Berry Wiggins. Berry was one of the most tireless glass researchers any of us has ever known. He was a good friend and would always be able to help me or anyone else identify a piece of glass. He was one of the pioneers in Stretch Glass and other American glass research. Berry could identify a piece by the shape of a marie or some other obscure measurement. Berry authored and co-authored many books and sat on many "glass ID panels." When the panel is not sure about a piece of glass that comes into an identification event, Frank Fenton, Dr. Measell, Roy Ash, Carrie Domitz or myself will turn to one another and say, "Berry would have known this one." We all miss him.

I never had the fortune of meeting William Heacock. He passed away one week after my first convention in 1988. From all accounts of those who knew him, I missed knowing a fine person and a great glass mind. Those of us today must be indebted to Bill and other researchers such a Ruth Webb Lee, Dr. Ruth Herrick, Berry Wiggins, and others. We should realize that they did not have the luxury of starting with all the information we have today. They started from "square one." Always remember and honor those who paved the way and keep their memories alive for future generations of collectors.

When I hear the word "collector," among the first individuals who come to mind is Bud Ashmore. Bud was a very close friend of the late Berry Wiggins. I admire Bud's knowledge on many types of glass, especially Northwood. I learn something new every time I see him. He has allowed many pieces of his glass to be photographed for a number of glass books.

I also must thank the owners of the Williamstown Antique Mall: Ed and Lori Radcliff, Jim and Sue Stage. In addition, former owners Ed and Shirley Lehew have been great friends and supporters. Their help in photographing and glass identification was invaluable. I also want to acknowledge former owners, the late Benton and Jill Ruppenthal. They were wonderful people and everyone who knew them misses their helpfulness and kindness.

Tom and Karin Sanders of Washington have been great friends and have extended their hospitality to me many times. Tom has a great glass mind. We talk on the phone several times in month and exchange information. He has helped many authors with their books and done seminars for many glass clubs. He is one of the best.

Roy Ash of Marietta, Ohio, has become one of my best friends in the last ten years. I am amazed at his knowledge on all types of glass and other areas such as the Civil War, coins, and jewelry. He is one of the best glass minds that I have had the pleasure to be associated with.

Lynn Welker of Ohio is one of the best glass minds in the country. He has been invaluable to many national clubs, such as Fenton, Heisey, and Cambridge. I have been pleased to call him a good friend for a number of years. His, his mother Mary, and late father Lyle's contributions to glass collecting have been invaluable.

Tom Burns, Bill Richards, and Billy Richards, Jr. of Burns Auction Service were incredibly helpful at the American Carnival Glass Club convention in 2004.They allowed me to photograph some wonderful glass during set up for the auction. They also helped make contacts with owners of some of the best carnival glass in the country so that I could get some wonderful pictures for this book.

Thanks to Steve Shorr and his great staff at Star Photo in Indianapolis. They provided excellent quality and fast service.

Fellow Schiffer authors, Randy and Debbie Coe, were kind enough to take some pictures of their glass and send me the slides.

Dave & Renee Shetlar, Ohio: Dave was co-author of the *American Iridescent Stretch Glass* book with John Madeley. Dave's knowledge of stretch glass is remarkable. He was invaluable in helping to check and verify the prices in the stretch glass chapter.

Margarett and Kenn Whitmyer from Ohio have been close friends and colleagues for many years. They have authored many important books on glassware and china. They are two of my favorite people.

Here are the others who, in large and small ways, contributed to this book:

Ed and Pat Anderson, Don and Dorene Ashbridge, Max and Sandy Blackmore, Carl Booker, Tom Burns, Randy and Debbie Coe, Bill Crowl, Pam Dick, Barton Dooley, Nick Duncan, Tim and Kathy Eicholz, John and Ann Fenton, Fenton Art Glass Museum, Frank M. Fenton, Maurice & Peggy Fulkerson, Art and Ellen Gilbert, Charles Griggs, Bob Grissom, Bruce Hill, Kill Creek Antiques, Melvin and Norma Lampton, Kevin Lavender, Ed and Shirley Lehew, Tom Limback, Terry L. Mackey, Jennifer Maston, Bill and Sharon Mizell, Chester and Debby Moody, Wayne and Beverly McKeehan, David and Debbie Neilsen, Loretta and John Nielsen , Oldfield Family, Gordon and Sue Phifer , Karen and Mike Pommier, Ed and Lori Radcliff, Dave and Linda Rash, Janet R. Reichling, Bill Richards, Billy Richards, Jr., Carole Richards, Byron and Grace Rinehart, Cheryl Robinson, Eileen and Dale Robinson, Harry Rosenthal, Jr., Carl and Fern Schroeder, David and Renee Shetlar, Arna Simpson, Douglas Siska, Arnold and Dorothy Snell, Mike Soper, Richard and Sara Speaight, Sue and Jim Stage, Jim and Pam Steinbach, Richard and Barbara Thorne, Neil and Eddie Unger, Evan Walker, Phil and Nancy Waln, Mary and Lynn Welker, Robert and Betty Wiles, Stacy and Desiree Wills

There have been so many other people that I have had the fortune to meet over the last eighteen years. There are hundreds of collectors and dealers who have given of their time and friendship. There are many who have become lifelong friends.

Thank you everyone!

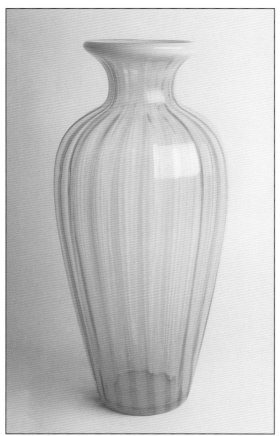

Introduction

I never in my wildest dreams thought that I would ever write a book. When John Walk said to me, "You should do a book on early Fenton rarities because you know more about it than I do and you know where the collections are," I thought, *excuse me*? However, when I would mention it to collectors, the response was unanimously positive. So here goes. I was asked by a number of people why I was writing this book now, and why would people want to see this book. My answer was simple. I'm writing this book for present collectors, and future collectors years from now. Hopefully, in twenty or thirty years, someone will look at this book and say, "I'm glad Tom took the time all those years ago to photograph this rare and wonderful glass for us to see today." It's that simple.

My wish is that all Fenton collectors, and all glass lovers and collectors, will enjoy this book. I have been so privileged to meet and become lifelong friends with so many Fenton collectors over the last eighteen years. Even more privileged to have been invited into their homes to see and photograph these rare and wonderful pieces. It has been a pleasure and honor to have become friends with the Fenton family and their employees. Thank you for making this wonderful glass for the last 100 years.

In organizing the chapters, I tried to do it in a somewhat chronological order. There are, of course, some treatments and styles that will overlap in some time periods. For example, with Dancing Ladies pieces being so popular, I put them together in one chapter instead of placing some in with opaques, others with noniridized, and more in opalescent. I tried to make the organization of the chapters as easy and as self-explanatory as possible. I hope the readers find it easy to locate pieces of their particular interest; I also hope readers find this book an enjoyable read.

Pricing and Values

Compiling a price guide for any book is one of the most difficult and thankless things any author will ever do. Just ask any author or try it yourself sometime. It used to be fairly simple to understand pricing before 1995 (Before Ebay). The main outlets for buyers were shows, antique shops, and malls. Buyers who might only pay 300 dollars for a piece in a shop, might now bid $400 or more on Ebay if they believe other buyers are interested. Most of the pieces pictured in this book may come available once every few years, once every ten years or not at all. I have tried to be fair in my pricing, taking into account prices that I have seen pieces sell for at shows, conventions, privately, and on the Internet. My advice to any serious collector is, you have to ask yourself these questions:

- When was the last time I saw this piece ... or have I *ever* seen one?
- When might I be lucky enough to see one again ... or *will* I ever see one again, and how much higher price will it be then?
- How many are known?
- If I walk away from this piece for a few dollars over what I think it is worth, will I be kicking myself tomorrow?

In the end, you will have to make your own decision as to how much it would be worth. If you have ever passed up a rare piece, you know how regrets feel. I know this old saying is old, but the time to buy a rare piece of Fenton IS when you see it.

When pricing, I have tried to use ranges whenever possible. There are, however, some pieces that are so rare that the sky would be the limit if they ever came to market. In these cases, I have listed it as price "und" for undetermined.

There are also some pieces that I have priced with a plus, for example $600+. This means that $600 would be the price that a serious collector, or someone with an acute knowledge of Fenton, would not walk away from when buying the piece. The plus symbol indicates that the piece is unusual enough that those serious collectors might also pay a good deal more than $600 for the item, especially if they felt they might not see the piece again. You will have to decide how much higher the "+" takes the price.

Even though I picture mostly single candlesticks, all prices are for a PAIR! In most cases and opinions, a single is worth about forty percent of a pair. I wish you all great hunting for pieces of rare Fenton Glass. I'm sure new and exciting pieces will turn up. Please let me know if you find a rare piece in a rare color or treatment. I would love to document it for future publications.

The prices found in the captions are in United States dollars. Prices vary immensely based on the location of the market, the venue of the sale, the rarity of the items, and the enthusiasms of the collecting community. Prices in the Midwest differ from those in the West or East, and those at specialty shows or auctions will differ from those in dealer's shops or through dealer's web pages.

All of these factors make it impossible to create absolutely accurate prices listings, but a guide to realistic pricing may be offered. Please note: these values are not provided to set prices in the antiques marketplace, but rather to give the reader a reasonable idea of what one might expect to pay for mint condition Fenton rarities.

The author and publisher assume no responsibility for any losses incurred through the use of prices in this book.

Chapter 1
Early, Opalescent, Custard

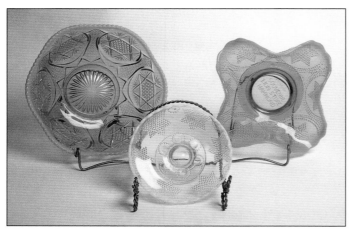

Three items showing different patterns: 10" Northern Star bowl, $45-55; 6" Beaded Star bowl, $35-45; and 8" Beaded Star and Swag with "Lion Store Adv. From Hammond, IN," $85-105. *Courtesy of Fenton Museum.*

Green Opalescent 7" Coin Spot and Buttons & Braids vases. Identified as Fenton due to the number of plumes (five) matching the known number for Fenton. Jefferson Buttons & Braids have seven plumes. These are the only ones known. $150-200 ea.

Green Opalescent Honeycomb and Clover water pitcher, $200-225.

Green Opalescent 4" Drapery spittoon whimsy, $75-100. *Courtesy of Fenton Museum.*

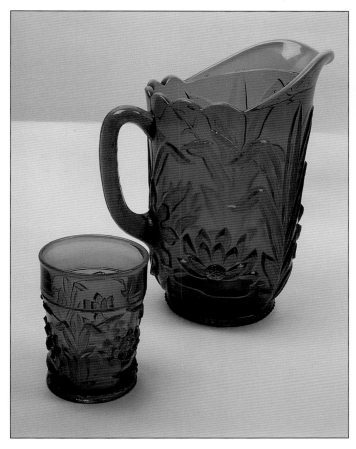

Amethyst Opalescent Water Lily & Cattails covered butter, $250-275; water pitcher, $300-325; Coin Spot tumbler, $30-35. *Courtesy of Fenton Museum.*

Amethyst Opalescent Water Lily & Cattails water pitcher, $300-325. Tumbler, $50-65 ea.

Green Opalescent 3" Water Lily & Cattails whimsy vase from a tumbler, $75-100. Marigold 8" Carnival Water Lily & Cattails vase, $450-550. *Courtesy of Fenton Museum.*

Amethyst Opalescent Water Lily & Cattails covered butter, $250-275.

Chocolate Idyll 7" vase, $500-600; 8" Marigold Idyll vase, $450-550. *Courtesy of Fenton Museum.*

Chocolate Water Lily & Cattails tumbler, $175+; pitcher, $1500+. *Courtesy of Fenton Museum.*

Cameo Opalescent hexagonal creamer & sugar, $250-200. *Courtesy of Fenton Museum.*

Chocolate Orange Tree powder box, $550-600. *Courtesy of Mike Soper.*

Various Custard Stains: #6 Blackberry Banded crimped (pink) vase; #1410 Orange Tree hatpin holder (nutmeg); Persian Medallion rose bowl (red) and #6 Blackberry Banded tulip (green) vase. Prices Und. *Courtesy of Fenton Museum.*

Chocolate Water Lily & Cattails 4 1/2" sauce bowl, $125-150. *Courtesy of Wayne & Beverly McKeehan.*

#1134 Cherry Scale table set: covered sugar, $125-150; covered butter, $175-200; spooner, $100-125; and creamer, $125-150.

#1412 Orange Tree mugs, transparent green, red, powder blue, milk, and custard.
Prices Und. *Courtesy of Mike Soper.*

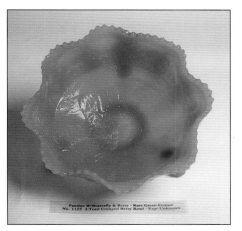

Nile Green 10" Panther three-footed
bowl. One known. Price Und. *Courtesy
of Fenton Museum.*

#599 Persian Blue table set, Banded Laurel: covered sugar, $70-80; covered butter,
$85-95; spooner, $45-50; creamer, $60-70. Author sold this set to Frank Fenton in 1996
for the Museum for $215.

#821 Ruby Cannonball pitcher & tumbler.
Pitcher, $175-225; Tumbler, $40-50.
Courtesy of Fenton Museum.

Assortment of three decorated Cannonball pitchers. Green, Crystal, and Amethyst.
$250-300 ea. *Courtesy of Fenton Museum.*

Chapter 2
Carnival Glass

Carnival glass is a completely different and specialized area than that of collecting other Fenton glass. There are many special nuances, such as shape, color, finish, and patterns. Market prices are much more volatile than other pieces of Fenton. Learning about Carnival glass takes years, involving much time and research. Novice collectors should educate themselves before buying expensive pieces. Study books and price guides, join clubs and follow trending. In other words, do your homework! Prices on these pieces are for examples in mint condition. Carnival Glass collectors are extremely selective, and rightly so when paying thousands of dollars for various pieces. Many of the pieces pictured here are examples with superior iridescence and finish. Pieces with good or average finish are in many cases worth much less.

Advertising/Souvenirs

State House of Indiana blue plate. $12,000+.

Marigold State House of Indiana plate, $14,000+.
Cobalt Illinois Soldiers & Sailors House plate, $2000+. *Courtesy of Fenton Museum.*

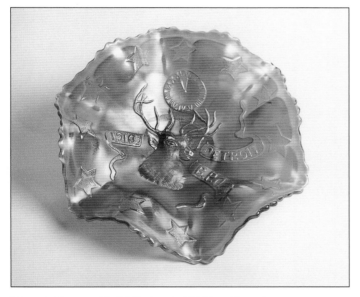

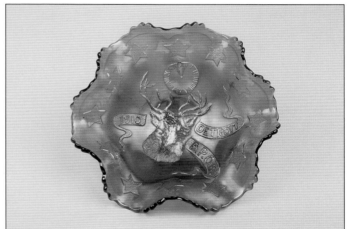

Green Detroit 1910 Elks bowl, $750+. *Courtesy of Mike Soper.*

Marigold Detroit 1910 Elks bowl, $9000+. Three known.
Courtesy of John & Loretta Nielsen.

1914 Parkersburg Elk bell,
$2000+. Cobalt 1914
Parkersburg Elks plate,
$2000+. Blue 1911 Atlantic
City Elks bell, $2000+.
Courtesy of Fenton Museum.

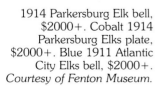

Cobalt Blue Grape & Cable bowl. "Compliments of Pacific Coast Mail Order House, Los Angeles." Price Und. *Courtesy of John & Loretta Nielsen.*

Blue 1911 Atlantic City Elks bowl, $750-1000. Blue 1914 Parkersburg Elks plate, $2000+. Green 1910 Detroit Elks bowl, $750+. *Courtesy of Fenton Museum.*

Detail of the interior of the Grape & Cable bowl.

Amethyst Utah Liquor Company plate, $750-900. Amethyst 1911 Birmingham Age Herald plate, $2200+. Amethyst "Eat Paradise Sodas" plate, $500+. *Courtesy of Fenton Museum.*

Marigold Hearts & Vines plate. "Compliments of Spector's Department Store." $1000+. *Courtesy of Stacy and Desiree Wills.*

Amethyst "Dreibus Parfait Sweets" handgrip plate, $1000+. Black plate – Price Und. Amethyst "Fern Brand Chocolates" handgrip plate, $1000+.

Bowls, Bonbons, and Compotes

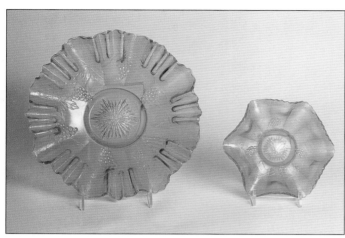

Celeste blue 10" vintage 3 in 1 bowl, $3000+. Celeste Blue 5" vintage bowl, $1000+. *Courtesy of Stacy & Desiree Wills.*

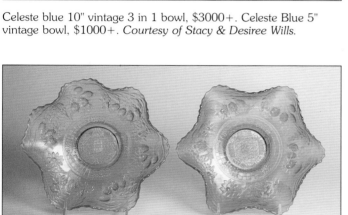

Ice green 9" Orange Tree bowl, $7500+. Celeste Blue 9" Orange Tree bowl, $6000+. *Courtesy of Stacy & Desiree Wills.*

#1414 Celeste Blue Pond Lily three-footed bowl (rare), $2000+. *Courtesy of Ed & Lori Radcliff.*

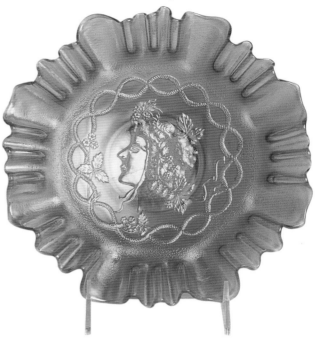

Marigold Goddess of Harvest bowl, $10,000+. *Courtesy of Evan Walker.*

Amethyst Goddess of Harvest bowl. $10,000+. *Courtesy of Fenton Museum.*

Marigold Hearts & Vines "Good Luck" bowl. $2000+. *Courtesy of Stacy & Desiree Wills.*

Blue Feather Stitch bowl, 9", $150-200. *Courtesy of Fenton Museum.*

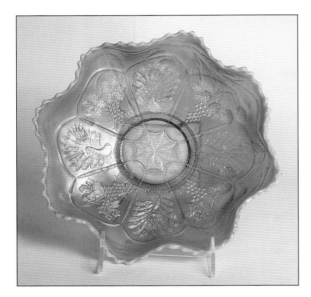

Aqua 9" Peacock & Grape bowl. Price Und.

Cobalt Blue "Peter Rabbit" bowl. $2000+. *Courtesy of Stacy & Desiree Wills.*

Red Dragon & Lotus bowl. Outstanding example, $800+.

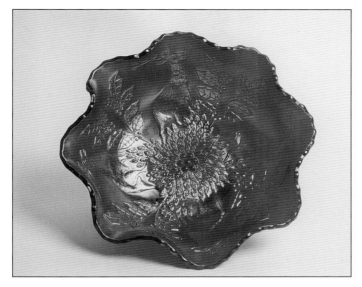

Red Stag & Holly spatula footed bowl, $1500+.

Red Peacock & Grape bowl, $750+; Red Holly Jack in the Pulpit hat, $600+.

Red Two Flowers spatula footed bowl, $4000+.

Red 5" acorn bowl, $500+; 10" Red Little Flowers bowl, $2000+.

Red Coin Spot 5" bowl, $700+. Red Vintage 10" bowl, $2000+.

Marigold Dragons Tongue three-footed bowl, $750+.
Courtesy of Fenton Museum.

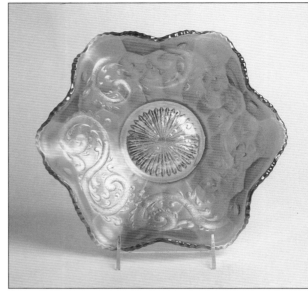

Vaseline Feathered Serpent bowl. One known.
Price Und. *Courtesy of Douglas Siska.*

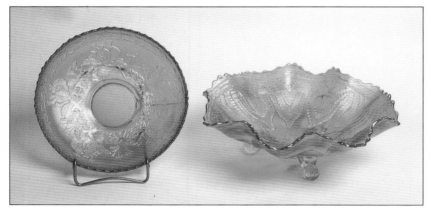

Marigold Coral bowl, $150-200; Marigold Dragons Tongue
three-footed bowl, $750+. *Courtesy of Fenton Museum.*

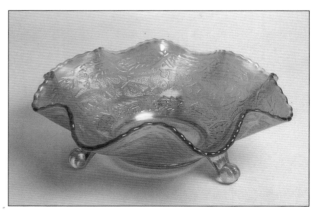

Marigold Little Fishes 10" footed bowl, $400-450.

Electric blue Butterfly & Berry fernery whimsy, $1000+.
Courtesy of Fenton Museum.

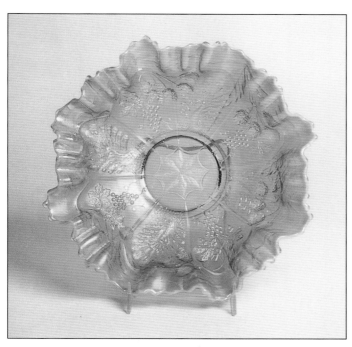

Vaseline Peacock & Grape 3 in 1 bowl, $500-750.

Aqua Stag & Holly 10" footed bowl, $500-750.

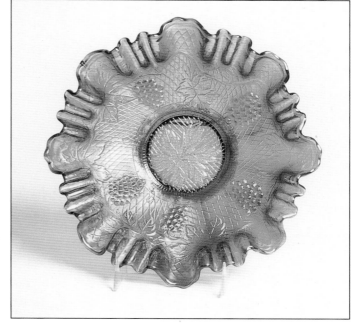

Amethyst Concord 3 in 1 bowl, $350-425.

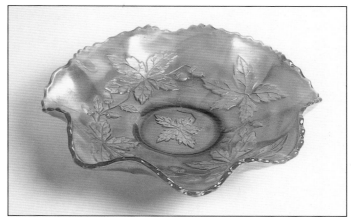

Powder blue 9" Vintage bowl, $1000+.
Courtesy of the Oldfield Family.

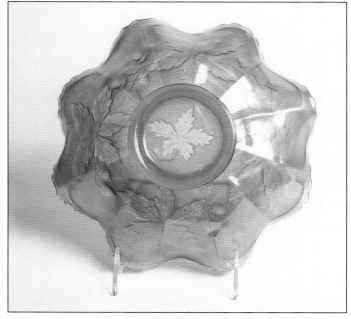

Reverse side of the powder
blue Vintage bowl.

Marigold Little Daisies 10" bowl, $500+.
Courtesy of Fenton Museum.

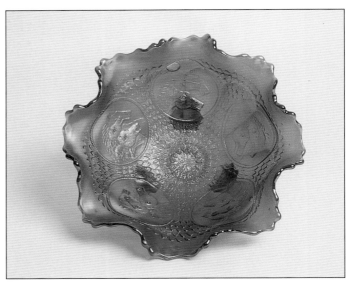

Green Horsehead 7" three-footed bowl, $500+.

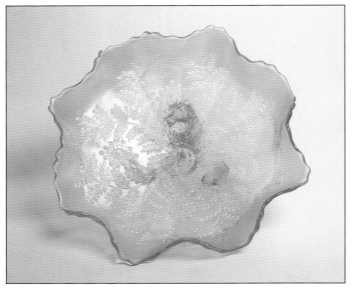

Marigold 10" fern bowl. Two known. Price Und.
Courtesy of Fenton Museum.

Side view of Horsehead bowl.

Aqua Horsehead rose bowl (rare) Price Und.
Courtesy of Arnold & Dorothy Snell.

Side view of aqua Horsehead rose bowl.

Red Peacock & Grape bowl, $1000+.

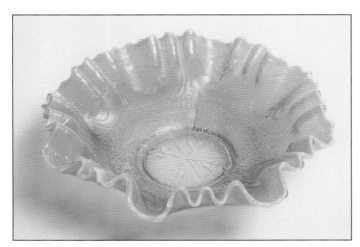

Vaseline Opalescent 10" Dragon & Lotus 3 in 1 bowl, $500+. *Courtesy of Fenton Museum.*

Green Hearts & Trees 11" three-footed bowl, $750+. *Courtesy of Mike Soper.*

Reverse side of the Green Hearts & Trees bowl showing the Butterfly & Berry exterior.

Green Orange Tree 10" three-footed fruit bowl, $750-1000. *Courtesy of Mike Soper.*

Green Grape & Cable 10" three-footed bowl with Persian Medallion interior, $500+.

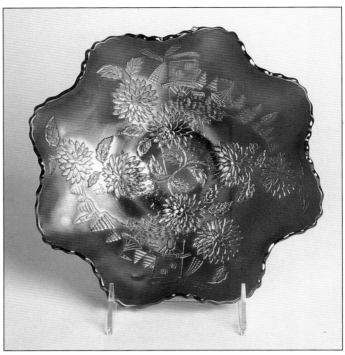

Red Chrysanthemum 10" bowl, $4000+. *Courtesy of Bruce Hill.*

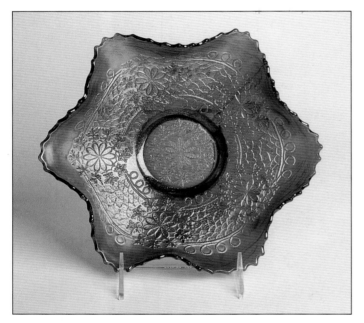

Lavender 10" Cherry Chain bowl. One known. Price Und.

Marigold yellow slag, Dragon & Lotus bowl. One known. Price Und. *Courtesy of Richard & Barbara Thorne.*

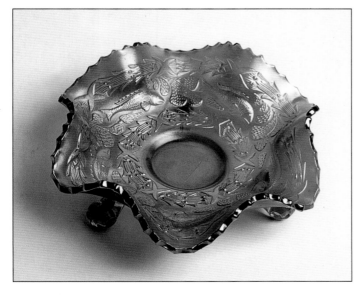

Aqua Little Fishes 5" three-footed bowl, $350-450. *Courtesy of Carl & Ferne Schroeder.*

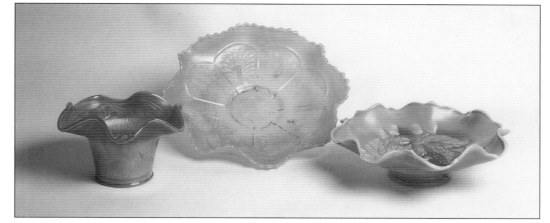

Moonstone 5" Banded Blackberry hat, $175-225. Peacock & Grape 9" bowl, $500-750. Acorn bowl, 5", $250-300. *Courtesy of Mike Soper.*

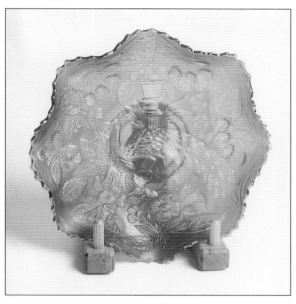

Persian Blue 10" Peacock & Urn bowl. $2000+. *Courtesy of Mike Soper.*

Blue Bird & Cherries 10" shallow bowl, $500. Blue 8" Ribbon Tie bowl, $350-400. *Courtesy of Fenton Museum.*

Exterior of the Peacock & Urn bowl.

White 10" Little Fishes three-footed bowl. (Rare.) $500+.

White 5" Kittens crimped bowl and round bowl. Prices Und.

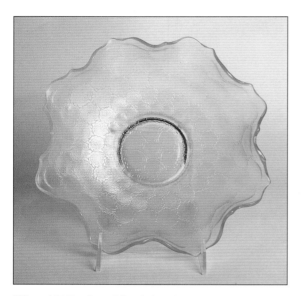

White 10" Feathered Stitch bowl. Price Und. *Courtesy of Stacy & Desiree Wills.*

Aqua Opalescent 5" Blackberry crimped hat, $700-800. Reverse Amberina Opalescent crimped hat, $700-1000. *Courtesy of Mike Soper.*

White 5" Iris compote, $200-250. White 10" Chrysanthemum three-footed ice cream shape bowl. $500+. *Courtesy of Mike Soper.*

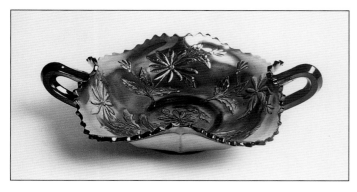

Blue Daisy two-handled bonbon, $150-200.
Courtesy of Mike Soper

Opaque blue Pond Lily two-handled bonbon, $1000+. Blue Illusion two-handled bonbon, $100-150. *Courtesy of Fenton Museum.*

Amberina Holly goblet compote, $500+.

Holly compotes together.

Amberina Red Holly goblet compote, $750-1000.

Pitchers, Tumblers, and Table Pieces

Amethyst Blackberry Block tankard, $1500+ (Extremely Rare).

Blue Lily of the Valley tumbler, $400-500; pitcher, $3000+.
Courtesy of Fenton Museum.

Blue Wine & Roses goblet and pitcher (rare). Prices Und.
Courtesy of John & Loretta Nielsen.

Blue Scale Band tumbler, $75-125 each; pitcher, $400-450.
Courtesy of John & Loretta Nielsen.

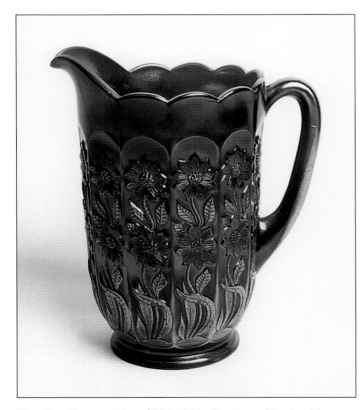

Blue Orange Tree scroll tankard, $1800+.
Courtesy of Ed & Lori Radcliff.

Blue Orange Tree Orchard pitcher, $1000-1300. Blue Orange Tree covered sugar, $200-250. Blue Orange Tree pitcher, $500-700. *Courtesy of Fenton Museum.*

Blue Ten Mums tumbler, $100-125; tankard pitcher, $1000+. *Courtesy of Fenton Museum.*

Blue Star Flower pitcher, $800-1200. *Courtesy of Fenton Museum.*

Blue Bouquet tumbler, $50-75;
pitcher, $400-475.

Blue Blueberry pitcher, $650-680; tumbler, $75-100. Marigold
Blueberry pitcher, $400-500; tumbler, $50-75.

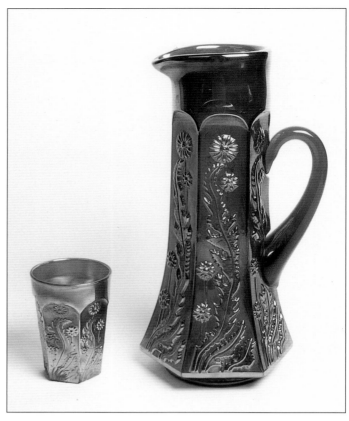

Green Paneled Dandelion tumbler, $75-100; tankard pitcher,
$1000-1200. *Courtesy of Fenton Museum.*

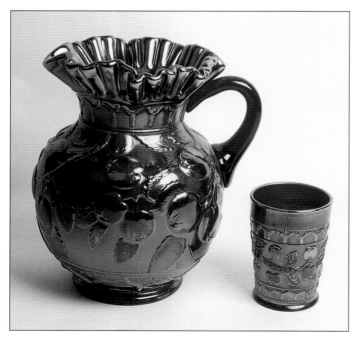

Blue Apple Tree pitcher, $800-1000; tumbler, $50-75.
(The fruit is actually a quince.)

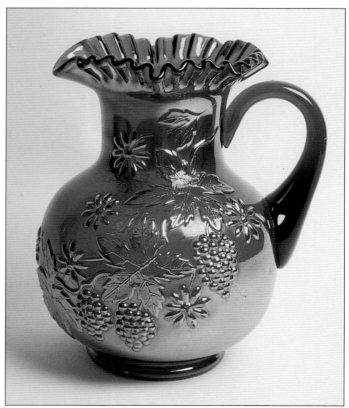

Green Bouquet pitcher, $700-800.

Green Blackberry Block
tumbler & tankard. Tumbler,
$125-150; tankard, $2000+.
Courtesy of Fenton Museum.

Marigold Zigzag enameled pitcher
& prism band tumbler. Pitcher,
$300-400; tumbler, $50-75.
Courtesy of Fenton Museum.

Green four piece Butterfly &
Berry table set (rare). Covered
sugar, $250-275; creamer, $200-
225; spooner, $175-225; butter
(complete), $300-350. Note:
Please contact the author if
anyone has a butter lid for sale.

29

Marigold Starflower pitcher, $7500+ (rare).
Courtesy of Stacy & Desiree Wills.

Marigold Scale bank tumbler, $25-50; pitcher, $100-125.
Courtesy of Fenton Museum.

Marigold Milady tumbler, $75-100; pitcher, $500-700.
Courtesy of Fenton Museum.

Marigold Leaf Tiers covered sugar, $100-150;
pitcher, $400-500. *Courtesy of Fenton Museum.*

White Butterfly & Berry pitcher. One known. Price Und. (If anyone has seen a tumbler, please contact the author.)

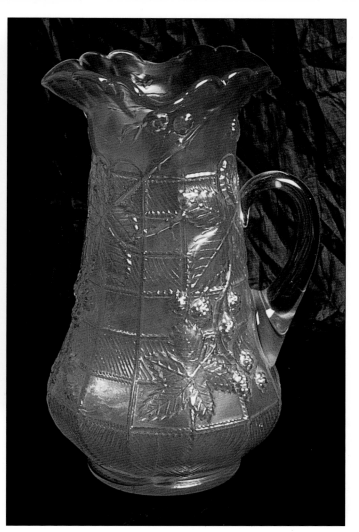

White Blackberry Block pitcher, $4000+.
Courtesy of Ed & Lori Radcliff.

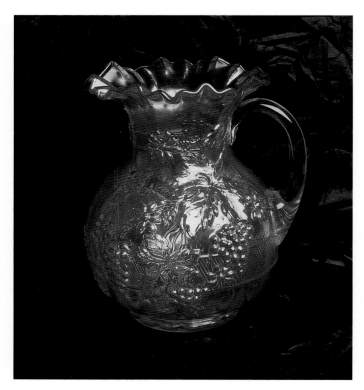

White Vintage pitcher, $750-1000.

White Orange Tree Orchard pitcher, $700-1000.

White Drapery Optic dianthus tankard, $500-700. Green Shasta Daisy tankard, $500-700. Amethyst Iris Band tankard, $750-1000. *Courtesy of Ed & Lori Radcliff.*

Marigold tumblers/various patterns: Dahlia, $75-100; Orange Tree Orchard, $75-100; Fluffy Peacock, $75-100; Water Lily & Cattails, $50-75. *Courtesy of Ed & Lori Radcliff.*

Various tumblers: Green Paneled Dandelion, $75-100; Blue Lattice & Grape, $100-150; Blue enameled Cherries, $75-100; Blue Apple Tree, $100-125; Green Butterfly & Fern, $75-100. *Courtesy of Ed & Lori Radcliff.*

Amber Honeycomb & Clover spooner, $100-150.
Courtesy of Mike Soper.

Tumblers: Marigold Leaf Tiers, $50-60;
Marigold Lattice & Grape, $450-600.

Tumblers: Green Vintage, $75-100; Marigold Leaf Tiers, $50-60; Blue Lily of the Valley, $400-500.

Plates

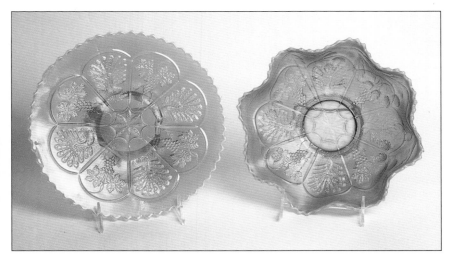

Marigold Peacock & Grape plate, $750-950; Aqua Opalescent Peacock & Grape bowl, $1000+. *Courtesy of Bob Grissom.*

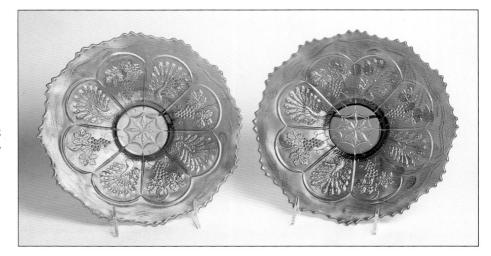

Green Peacock & Grape plate, $4500+; Amethyst Peacock & Grape plate, $5000+. *Courtesy of Bob Grissom.*

Marigold 9" Vintage plate, $700-800; Marigold 9" Coral plate, $1000+.

Marigold 6" Cherry Chain plate, $150-200; Blue 9" Orange Tree, $400-600; Marigold 4" Kittens cup plate, $200-225; Blue 7" Vintage plate, $150-200; Marigold Little Flowers chop plate, $750-1000. *Courtesy of Ed & Lori Radcliff.*

Amethyst 9" Dragon & Lotus plate, $4000+.
Courtesy of Bob Grissom.

Blue Orange Tree plate, $400-600; Marigold Little Flowers chop plate, $750-1000. *Courtesy of Ed & Lori Radcliff.*

Amethyst Captive Rose plate, $750-1000.

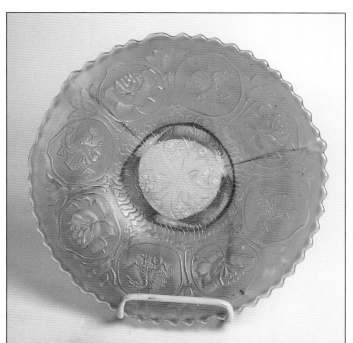

Marigold Dragon & Lotus plate, $2000+.
Courtesy of Bob Grissom.

Marigold 9" Coral plate, $1000+.

Marigold 10" three-footed Stag & Holly plate, $800-1000.
Courtesy of the Oldfield Family, England.

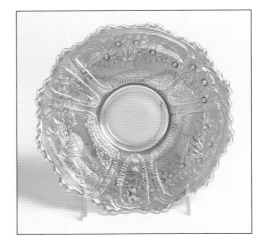

Marigold 6" Sailboats plate, $175-225.
Courtesy of Ed & Lori Radcliff.

Cobalt Peter Rabbit plate, $3000-4000 (One sold on Ebay in September 2004 for, $5000.) *Courtesy of Fenton Museum.*

Black Amethyst 10" Holly plate, $2000+.
Courtesy of Ed & Lori Radcliff.

Green Peter Rabbit plate,
$3000-4000.

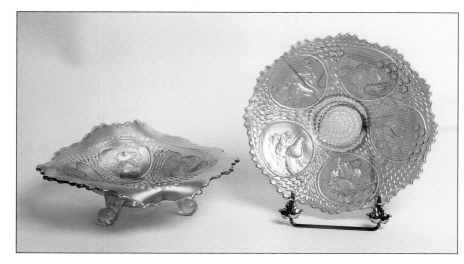

Vaseline Horsehead Jack in the Pulpit three-footed bowl, $400-500; Marigold 7" Horsehead plate, $200-300. *Courtesy of Fenton Museum.*

White Cherry Chain plate, $500-600; White 10" Butterfly & Berry master bowl, $900+. Note: These bowls have been reproduced in a White Opalescent and other colors.

Left: Original Red Holly plate. Right: Shown for comparison with a Red Holly plate made for Mr. Frank Fenton's 85th birthday in 2000.

Red 10" Holly plate. "Outstanding piece." One known. Price Und.

Amethyst Bird & Cherries chop plate. "This is one of the best pieces of Fenton or any Carnival glass." $20,000+. *Courtesy of Stacy & Desiree Wills.*

Amethyst Captive Rose plate, Price Und.; Green Concord plate, $6000+. *Courtesy of Stacy & Desiree Wills.*

Marigold 9" Water Lily plate, Price Und.; Fantail 9" plate with Butterfly & Berry exterior, $6000+. *Courtesy of Stacy & Desiree Wills.*

Green Persian Medallion plate, $8000+; Marigold Persian Medallion plate, $3000+. *Courtesy of Stacy & Desiree Wills.*

Marigold 7" Peacock & Dahlia plate, $1000+; Amethyst 10" Lotus & Grape plate, $7000+. *Courtesy of Stacy & Desiree Wills.*

Marigold 9" Thistle plate, $9000+; Green 7" Thistle plate, $7000+. *Courtesy of Stacy & Desiree Wills.*

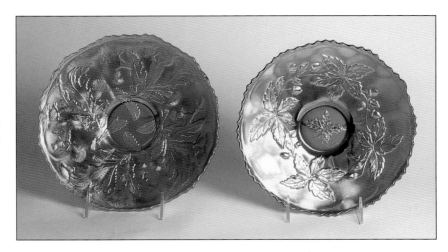

Marigold Little Flowers chop plate, $750-1000.
Courtesy of Ed & Lori Radcliff.

Amethyst 10" Concord plate, $2800+.

Green 10" Thistle plate, $4000-4400+.

Marigold Lotus & Thistle
whimsy plate, $500+.

Vases

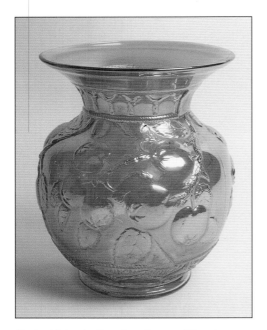

Marigold Apple Tree flared vase. (Rare.) $1500+.

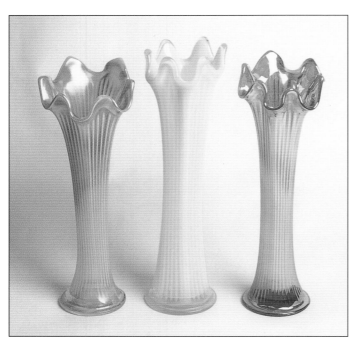

Fine rib vases: Vaseline Opalescent Iridized, $1500-1800; Vaseline Opalescent, noniridized, $200-225; Amber Opalescent, $1500-1600. *Courtesy of Mike Soper.*

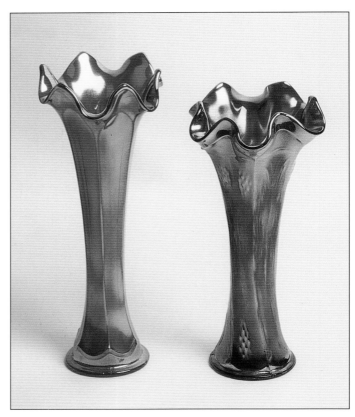

Red Panels vase, $500-550; Red Butterfly & Berry vase, $700-800.

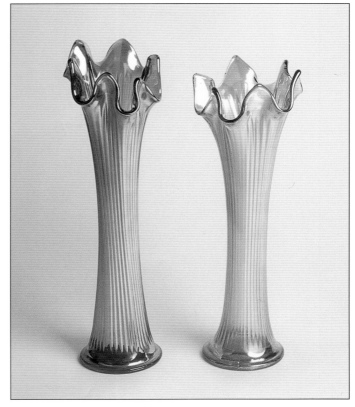

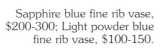

Sapphire blue fine rib vase, $200-300; Light powder blue fine rib vase, $100-150.

Marigold 19" Diamond Rib plunger base funeral vase, $2500-2700; Marigold Diamond Rib jardinière, $1000-1200. *Courtesy of Ed & Lori Radcliff.*

Red Butterfly & Berry swung vase, $700-800; Green Butterfly novelty, Price Und.; Marigold 5" Butterfly & Berry plate, $750-950. *Courtesy of Fenton Museum.*

#400 Red 6" vase, $500+; #500 Red rolled bonbon, $500+.

Plunger base 19" Amethyst Rustic funeral vase, $2000+; Standard Amethyst 19" Rustic funeral vase, $1000-1200. *Courtesy of Ed & Lori Radcliff.*

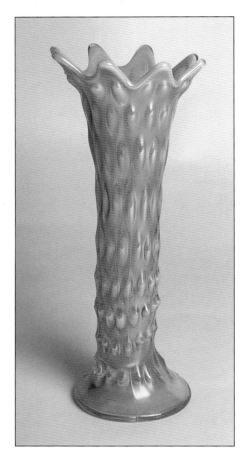

White 7" Rustic vase, $75-100. White 19" Rustic standard funeral vase, Price Und. *Courtesy of Douglas Siska.*

Peach 12" Opalescent Rustic vase, Price Und.

White Carnival Opalescent 10" Peacock vase, $2250+. *Courtesy of Mike Soper.*

White Standard funeral vase, $900-1000; White Plunger base Rustic funeral vase, $1500-2000. *Courtesy of Ed & Lori Radcliff.*

Blue Rustic Plunger base funeral
vase, $2500-3000. *Courtesy of
Don & Dorene Ashbridge.*

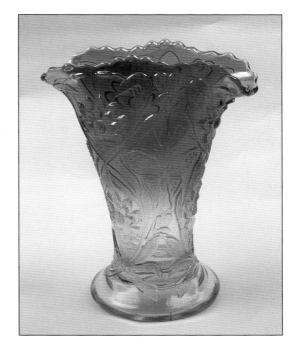

Marigold 6" Water Lily & Cattails flared rolled
vase, $550-600. *Loaned to the Fenton Museum
by Millie Coty.*

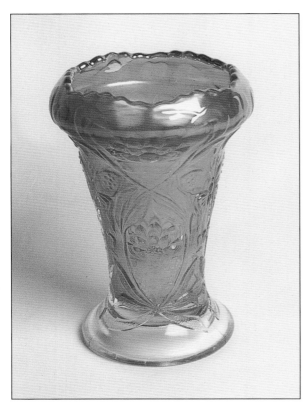

Marigold Water Lily & Cattails cupped vase, $800+.
Courtesy of Mike Soper.

Amethyst Long Thumbprint vase with 1899
Indian head penny in base, Price Und.

Whimsies

Cobalt Butterfly & Berry tri-cornered sauce or berry bowl, $2000+.

Marigold & Blue Kittens spittoon, Prices Und.

Amethyst Butterfly & Berry spittoon from a 5" berry bowl, Price Und. Marigold Lattice spittoon tumbler whimsy, Price Und.

Back Row: Marigold Lattice & Grape tumbler vase; Marigold Water Lily & Cattails swung tumbler vase; Marigold Vintage tumbler spittoon bowl. Front Row: Amethyst Butterfly & Berry spittoon. Prices Und.

Marigold 7" Water Lily & Cattails spittoon from a master berry, $500-600; Marigold Water Lily & Cattails swung tumbler vase. Price Und.

Marigold Smooth Rays spittoon bowl, $300-400.
Courtesy of Robert & Betty Wiles.

Orange Tree whimsy card tray from a punch cup.

Amethyst plate made out of a Vintage Fernery,
$1500+. *Courtesy of Ed & Lori Radcliff.*

Blue whimsy plate out of a Vintage Fernery, $1500+.
Courtesy of Mike Soper.

Blue Butterfly & Berry cupped master berry, $500-600; Marigold
Water Lily & Cattails swung tumbler vase whimsy, Price Und.

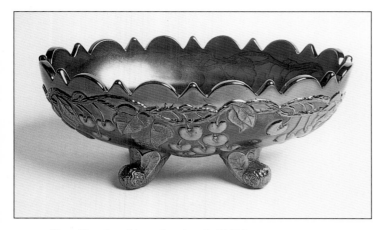

Blue Cherries oblong fruit bowl, $2000+.

Amethyst 10" Grape & Cable basket, $2500+.

Amethyst large Diamond Rib ruffled jardinière, $2500+.
Courtesy of Ed & Lori Radcliff.

Green large Diamond Rib straight jardinière, $2500+.
Courtesy of Terry Mackey.

Marigold Lattice & Grape swung tumbler vase, $500+.
Courtesy of Ed & Lori Radcliff.

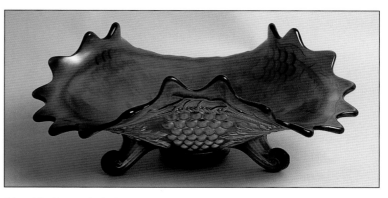

Blue 10" Grape & Cable tri-colored bowl made from the fruit bowl, $1000+.

Blue Orange Tree ruffled punch bowl base, $1000+; Marigold Basket Weave swung vase, $1000+.

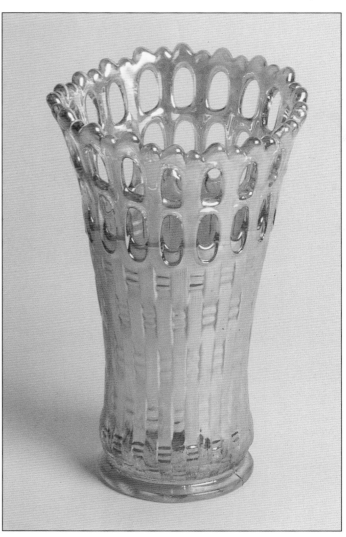

Marigold Basket Weave whimsy swung vase, $1000+.

47

Novelties, Epergnes, and Punch Sets

Butterfly novelties – Back Row: Marigold satin, $800-1000; Marigold radium, $800-1000; Clambroth, $800-900; blue, $1200-1400.
Front Row: Green, Vaseline, & Aqua. Prices Und.

Marigold, $200-250; Blue, $250-300; Green, $250-300; Amethyst, $250-300. *Courtesy of Ed & Lori Radcliff.*

Vintage epergnes – Green, $250-300; Amethyst, $250-300. *Courtesy of Ed & Lori Radcliff.*

Marigold Vintage epergne, $200-250.
Blue Vintage epergne, $250-300. *Courtesy of Ed & Lori Radcliff.*

White Orange Tree loving cup, $400-500. White Orange Tree hatpin holder, Price Und. *Courtesy of Stacy & Desiree Wills.*

Marigold Butterfly & Berry hatpin holder, $1200-1500; Blue Butterfly & Berry hatpin holder, $1500-2000.

Blue Kittens cereal bowl, $500-750.
Blue Kittens ruffled bowl, $500-750.

Marigold Orange Tree hatpin holder with open whimsy top, $600+. *Courtesy of Mike Soper.*

Blue Kittens spooner (toothpick), $250-275.
Blue Kittens cup & saucer, $1000-1200.

49

Blue noniridized Daisy cut bell, Price Und. Marigold Carnival Daisy cut bell, $500-600. *Courtesy of Fenton Museum.*

Amethyst Wreath of Rose
Left: Punch cup, Vintage interior, $50-75.
Right: Punch cup, Persian Medallion interior, $50-75; punch bowl with Persian Medallion interior & base, $1000-1200. *Courtesy of Ed & Lori Radcliff.*

Green Orange Tree punch bowl & base, Price Und. *Courtesy of Fenton Museum.*

Brick red 10" Grape & Cable bowl with Persian Medallion interior, $1000+. *Courtesy of Mike Soper.*

Amethyst Vintage rose bowl, $150-200.
Courtesy of Fenton Museum.

Root beer Dragon & Lotus bowl, Price Und.
Courtesy of Richard Barbara Thorne.

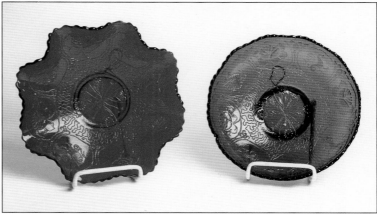

Red Dragon & Lotus bowl, Price Und. Root beer Dragon & Lotus bowl, Price Und. *Courtesy of Richard Barbara Thorne.*

Blue 10" Peacock & Urn plate, Price Und.
Red Orange Tree mug, Price Und.

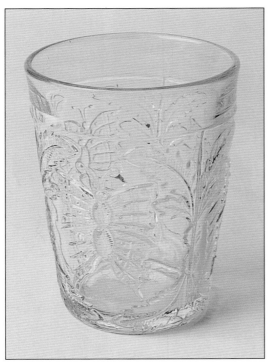

Crystal Butterfly & Fern tumbler. Price Und.

Amethyst Paneled Dandelion tumbler, Price Und.

Crystal Butterfly & Fern tumbler. Red Orange Tree mug. Prices Und.

Black Rustic vase, $100-125. Green Basket Weave bowl, $45-50. Red Amberina base, $60-75. Red Holly crimped bonbon, $100-125. *Courtesy of Mike Soper.*

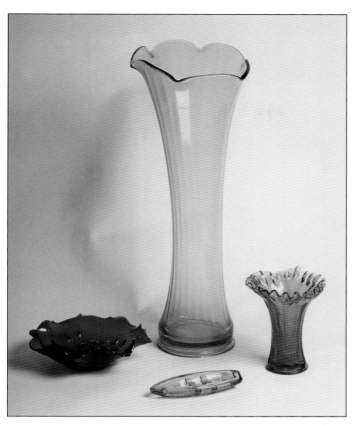

Crystal Peacock & Grape bowl. Price Und.
Courtesy of Stacy & Desiree Wills.

Amber 5" acorn bowl, $50-65; Amber 16" swung paneled vase, $75-100; Amber canoe ashtray, $25-30; Amber 6" Butterfly & Berry vase, $50-75. *Courtesy of Mike Soper.*

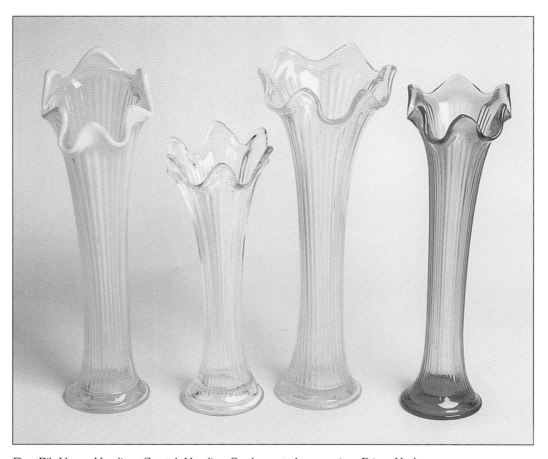

Fine Rib Vases: Vaseline, Crystal, Vaseline Opalescent, Aquamarine. Prices Und.

Chapter 3
Stretch Glass

Amber

Amber color in Stretch Glass is extremely rare.
There are not more than a half dozen pieces known.

#660 bowl, $60-75; #660 bowl, $60-75.

#1668 8" flip vase, $150-175.

Aquamarine

#349 10" bowl, $150-200; #1533A comport, $150-200.

Celeste Blue

Celeste Blue logo sign, $500+.

Dolphin oval-footed nut cup (rare). One other known with original label. $800-1000. *Courtesy of Carole Richards.*

#202 five piece ashtray set, $175-225.
Courtesy of Janet R. Reichling.

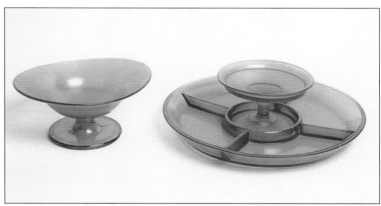

#923 flared oval comport, $55-65; #1647 sweet meat set, $300-400. *Courtesy of Fenton Museum.*

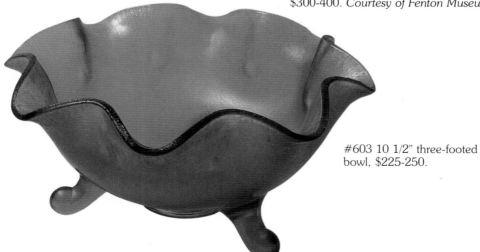

#603 10 1/2" three-footed bowl, $225-250.

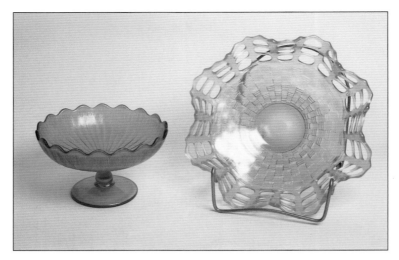

Stippled Rays compote, $375-325; #1093 Basket Weave bowl, $225-275. *Courtesy of Fenton Museum.*

#53 puff box, $100-125; #56 cologne, $200-225; #59 cologne, $175-200; #57 puff box, $95-110; #1502 tray, $100-125. *Courtesy of Janet R. Reichling.*

Size comparison: 55 1/2 Celeste cologne, $400-450; possibly Fenton cologne. (This is the first one the author has seen. It is smaller than the 7" #55 1/2.) *Courtesy of Dave & Linda Rash.*

Vase with cutting and base, 7 1/2".
Vase, $150-200; base, $125-150.
Courtesy of Fenton Museum.

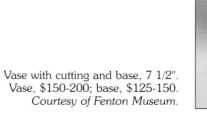

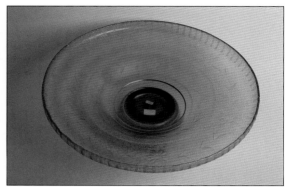

#1532 Celeste Blue Stretch 1/2 lb. dolphin candy, $125-150; #10 footed covered candy, $225-250; #543 flat covered bonbon, $75-95. *Courtesy of Dave & Linda Rash.*

#647 14" bowl with three different cuttings, $150-175.

Punch cup, $200-225; #1502 cup without Diamond Optic, $200-225; cup-plain, $50-75 ea.

Detail of the three different types of cuttings.

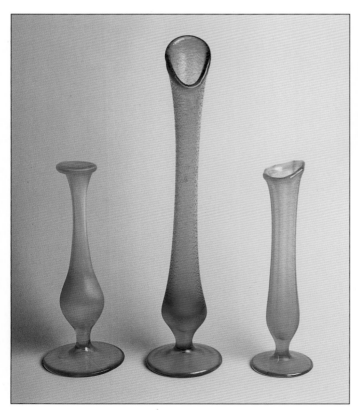

#99 7" flat top bud vase, $50-65; #251 bud vase, swung, 12", $45-60; #251 bud vase, 7", $40-55.

#750 Octagonal 9 1/2" bowl. $200-225. *Courtesy of Charles Griggs.*

Cobalt Blue

Fenton Cobalt Stretch is very rare.

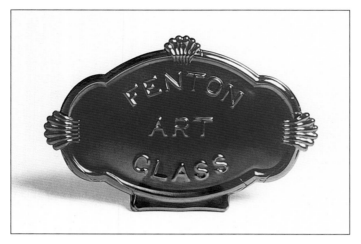

Logo sign. (As far as anyone knows, including Frank Fenton, this is the only one known. Known in green, blue, and topaz.) Price Und. *Courtesy of Ed & Lori Radcliff.*

#640 7" bowl, $175-200; #647, #604 10" bowl, $400-475; #232 candlestick, $500+ pair.

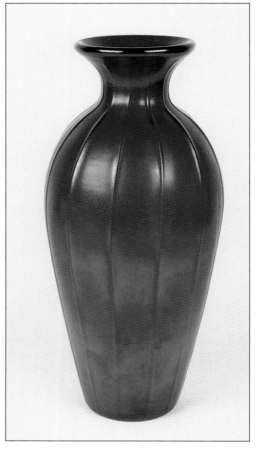

#891 vase, $800+.

Florentine Green

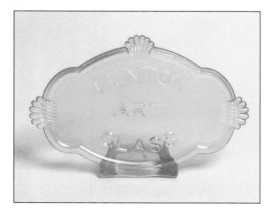

Logo sign, $500+. *Courtesy of Fenton Museum.*

#1093 8" Basket Weave bowl. $225-250. *Courtesy of Mike Soper.*

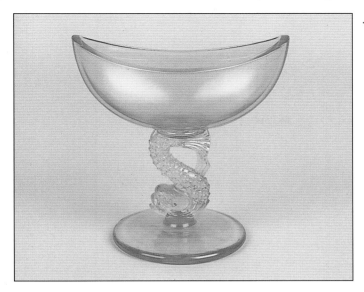

Dolphin footed oval nut cup, $600+.

Pitcher, 9 1/2", $225-250; tumbler, $45-55.
Courtesy of Gordon & Sue Phifer.

#57 puff box, $75-95; #55 cologne, $200-250; #54 puff box,
$125-150. *Courtesy of Janet R. Reichling.*

#2 creamer & sugar with cobalt handles, $200-250 pr.
Courtesy of Fenton Museum.

#556 cigarette holder, $150-200; #215 grape juice pitcher,
$225-275; logo sign, $500+. *Courtesy of Fenton Museum.*

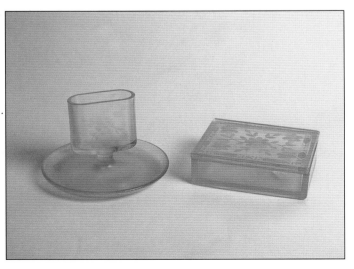

#556 cigarette holder, $175-200; #655 cigarette box with
cutting, $200-250. *Courtesy of Janet R. Reichling.*

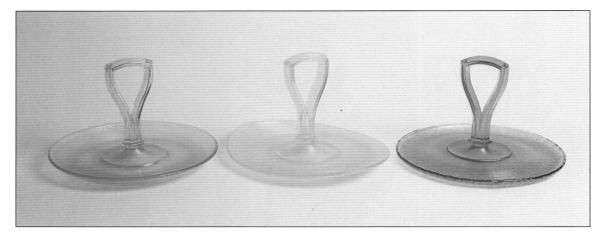

#318 oval butter balls: Florentine, $85-100; Topaz, $85-125; Celeste Blue, $85-100. *Courtesy of Janet R. Reichling.*

#923 mayonnaise & ladle, $75-95 set; #6403 sherbet & under plate, $45-55 set; #923 Velva mayo, $55-65. Courtesy of Janet R. Reichling.

#556 Florentine cigarette holder; #556 Velva Rose; #554 Marigold. $175-200 each. *Courtesy of Janet R. Reichling.*

Toothpick holders, 2 5/8": Florentine green, $250-300; Wisteria, $275-350. *Courtesy of Janet R. Reichling.* (Also found in Celeste & Topaz. Velva Rose reported and one known in Persian Pearl.)

#570 fan vase with black ship decoration, $100-125; #621 cupped 8" vase with cutting, $125-165. *Courtesy of Fenton Museum.*

Vases: #612 6" Florentine flared, $55-60; #1502 8" Celeste Diamond Optic, $95-125; #610 5" Wisteria cupped, $95-125. *Courtesy of Janet R. Reichling.*

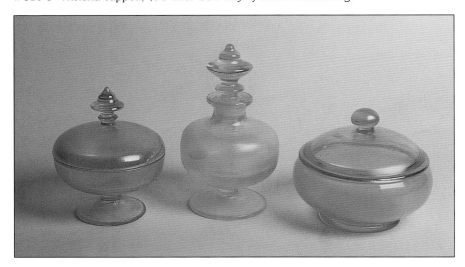

#57 puff box, $75-95; #56 Topaz cologne, $100-250; puff box, $100-125. *Courtesy of Janet R. Reichling.*

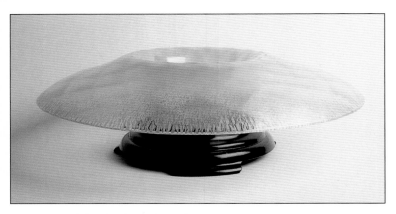

#1502 bowl, 13", $125-150.

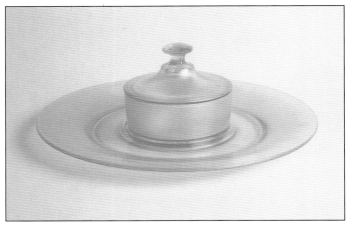

Covered bonbon on tray. (These were first thought to be US Glass until the covered bonbon showed up in Cameo Opalescent.) $150-225.

#1502 Diamond Optic dolphin fan vase (rare with Diamond Optic), $250-300; #1615 basket, $225-275; #1502 6" flared vase, $55-75.

#1522 bowl, 10", 3 in 1 crimp with marigold spray over Florentine green. (One known.) Price Und.

#215 grape juice tumbler & pitcher. Tumbler, $50-60; pitcher, $175-225.

#9 1 lb. covered candies showing different cuttings. $65-95 ea.

#2 creamer & sugar with cobalt handles, $200-250; #55 cologne, $175-225;
#57 puff box, $75-100; #55 1/2 cologne, $250-300; #844 flower finial
candy, $275-325. *Courtesy of Gordon & Sue Phifer.*

#59 cologne, $175-200; #56 cologne, $175-225; #55 1/2 perfume, $350-400;
#55 perfume, $200-250; #57 puff box, $75-85. *Courtesy of Janet R. Reichling.*

Marigold on Opalescent lamp shade, $100-150.
Courtesy of Janet R. Reichling.

#55 & #55 1/2 perfumes. (#55 1/2 has a flower top.) Jade #55 1/2, $300-400; Marigold #55, $200-250; Wisteria #55, $300-350; Celeste #55, $225-250; Celeste #55 1/2, $350-400. Prices reflect a "mint condition" dauber.

#923 Marigold nut cup, $45-55; #554 round cigarette holder, $175-225. *Courtesy of Janet R. Reichling.*

#2 Grecian Gold creamer & sugar with cobalt handles, $200-250;
#200 guest set, $325+. *Courtesy of Janet R. Reichling.*

Four Ring Grecian Gold pitcher with cutting cobalt handle,
$350-400; tumbler, $75-85. *Courtesy of Janet R. Reichling.*

#756 6" octagonal plate, $20-25; #403 sherbet, $15-20; plate,
$10-15; on #630 – 8 3/4" plate, $35-35.
6 1/2" round plate with Laurel leaf border (usually seen on an
octagonal plate), $30-35. *Courtesy of Janet R. Reichling*

#56 Topaz cologne, $200-250; #60 Marigold bath salt jar, $225-250; #56 Marigold cologne, $175-225.

Persian Pearl

#2 creamer & sugar with cobalt handles, $225-300 pr.; #200 guest set, $450+. *Courtesy of Janet R. Reichling.*

#893 ginger jar, base and lid, $350-400; A 6" bowl with spatula feet (rare), Carnival glass shape, $125-150.

Label on the bottom of the 7 1/2" vase.

A 7 1/2" vase with black dancing nymphs decoration. $225-275. *Courtesy of Gordon & Sue Phifer.*

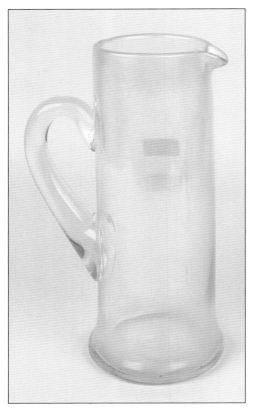

#1620 Plymouth basket, $400-500; #2000 Pineapple bowl, $700+. *Courtesy of Fenton Museum.*

#215 grape juice pitcher, $250-350 (rare color). *Courtesy of Bill Crowl.*

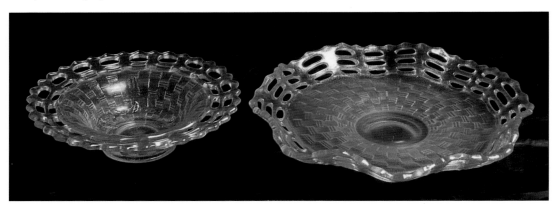

#1091 6" bowl with rare flat top, $225-275; #1093 8" bowl, $200-225. *Courtesy of Mike Soper.*

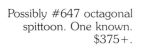

Possibly #647 octagonal spittoon. One known. $375+.

#573 vase with "KKK" cutting, $125-175.

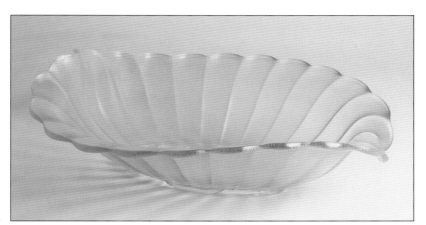

#1663 12" tulip bowl, $150-175.

#3 creamer & sugar, $100-150 pr.

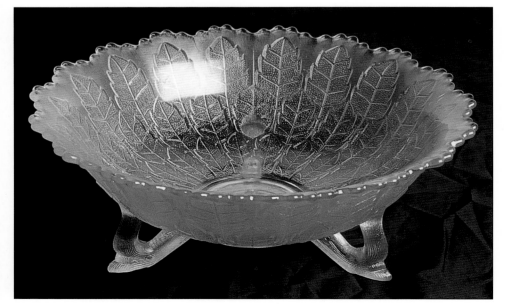

#1790 Leaf Tiers bowl.
One known. $350-450.

Red

Red Stretch is the most desirable color. Prices have escalated in the last few years due to its gaining popularity with Carnival glass collectors.

#604 Red punch bowl with base. (The last three of these that have come up at Carnival Glass convention auctions have sold for $3500-4500.) *Courtesy of Janet R. Reichling.*

#736 1 lb. candy jar, $800+.

#1504A three dolphin 7" bowl. Three known. (This is a rare & most desirable piece of Fenton Stretch.) $2000+. *Courtesy of Phil & Nancy Waln.*

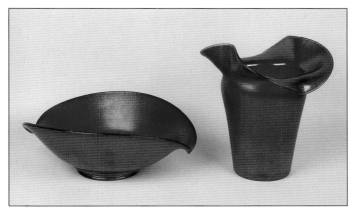

#600 oval 8" whimsy bowl, $800+; 8" whimsy vase, $800+.

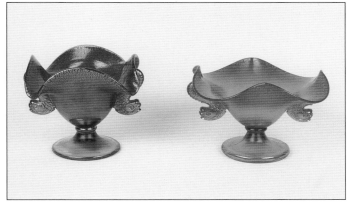

#1533A SGS (Stretch Glass Society) piece, c. 1994, $45 ea.;
#1533A dolphin bonbon, $1200+.

#604 bowls showing two different bases. Celeste Blue with shoulder.
Ruby without shoulder. Blue, 500+; Ruby, $800+.

Detail of the #604 bowls.

Tangerine

#9 covered bonbon, $275-350; #10 bonbon, $275-350.

#643 covered bonbon, $150-200.

#66 Lemon tray (only a few known), $175-225; #200 guest set, $800+. *Courtesy of Janet R. Reichling.*

#200 guest sets: Tangerine, $800+; Persian Pearl with cobalt handle, $450+; Grecian Gold with cobalt handle, $325+. *Courtesy of Janet R. Reichling.*

#847 vases showing the color extremes of Tangerine and the different shapes. $125-150 ea.

#66 Lemon tray, $175-225; #3 creamer, $125-150; #316 cheese comport,
$100-125; #314 candlestick, $125-150 pr. *Courtesy of Gordon & Sue Phifer.*

#3 creamer & sugar, $200-300 pr.; #2 creamer & sugar,
$300-450 pr. *Courtesy of Janet R. Reichling.*

#53 puff box (one known), $450+. *Courtesy of Charles Griggs.*

#53 puff box, $450+; #1502 cup, $200-225. *Courtesy of Charles Griggs.*

#573 8" rolled rim vase, $150-175. *Courtesy of Charles Griggs.*

Topaz

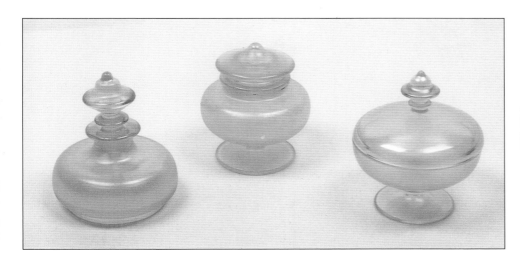

#59 cologne, $175-250; #60 bath salts jar, $225-275; #57 puff box, $75-95. *Courtesy of Gordon & Sue Phifer.*

#55 1/2 cologne, $350-450; #56 cologne, $200-250; #55 cologne, $225-275; #53 perfume, $150-200. *Courtesy of Janet R. Reichling.*

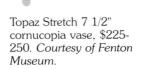

Topaz Stretch 7 1/2" cornucopia vase, $225-250. *Courtesy of Fenton Museum.*

Cup & saucer, $125-150 set; #1500 Velva ice tea, $200-250; #1502 octagonal plate, $30-35. *Courtesy of Janet R. Reichling.*

#630 shaving mug (there are less than a dozen of these known in all colors), $500+; covered bonbon, $75-100.

#918 12" high standard compote, $250-275.

#1647 two piece sweetmeat with metal trim, $400+.

Stippled Rays compotes:
Topaz, $150-225;
Grecian Gold, $150-225;
Velva Rose, $150-225.

Console set: #449 8 1/2" candles with cut ovals, $500+ pr.; #601 10" bowl, $250+.

Victorian Topaz

Listed as Stretch Glass, these pieces border on art glass. Pieces do not appear often.

4 Ring 5 3/8" high tumbler, $300-350; 4 Ring
8 1/4" high pitcher, $1800-2000.

Four Ring 8" vase, $800-1200.

Four Ring Curtain Optic pitcher, 9 1/4" high, $2000+; #222 pitcher,
10 1/4" high, $2000+; Four Ring 8 1/4" high pitcher, $2000-2500.

Vase with cobalt handles, 9", $1500-2000.

Four Ring 10" vase, noniridized, $800-900.
Courtesy of Charles Griggs.

Four Ring 8" vase with
cobalt edge, $1200-1500.

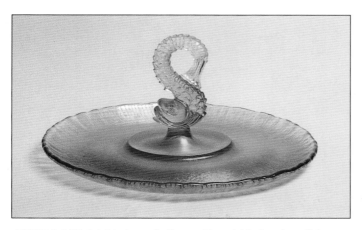

#1557 6 1/2" dolphin butterball tray. (Rare.) (Only a handful are known in green & Velva.) $400-600. *Courtesy of Thomas K. Smith.*

Mold # unknown. Puff box, 6" diameter, $200-225; #1623 dolphin Spiral Optic candle, $150-200 pr.

#222 Velva Rose tankard, $300-400; #222 tumbler, $60-80. *Courtesy of Charles Griggs.*

#1555 large Velva flowerpot and base, $150-225.

#923 nut cups: Velva Rose, $50-60; Topaz (flared), $55-60; Marigold, $45-50; Celeste, $45-50. *Courtesy of Janet R. Reichling.*

#53 colognes: Velva Rose Optic; Persian Pearl Optic; Florentine green without Optic, $125-175 ea. *Courtesy of Janet R. Reichling.*

#567 fan vase, $55-65; #1536 6" compote, $100-125; #100 6" Ring bowl, $50-75.

#3 creamer & sugar, $95-125 pr.

#318 Spiral Optic candles. (Rare with Optic.) $100-125 pr.

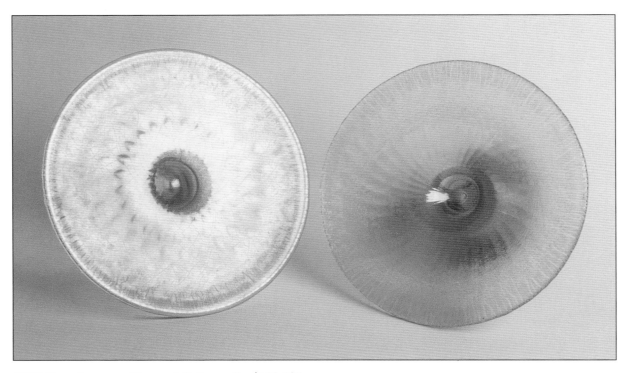

#318 Florentine green Diamond Optic candle, $100-125 pr.;
#318 Velva Spiral candle (for comparison).

Wisteria

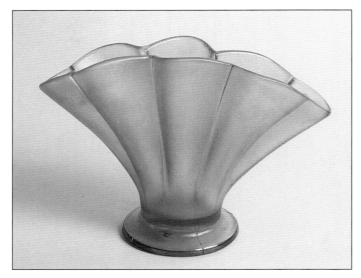

#847 fan vase in an unusual color. (Northwood used this color; however, this is a Fenton shape. The author has seen two or three pieces in this color.) $150-175. *Courtesy of Janet R. Reichling.*

#604 12" flared bowl and base. Bowl, $400+; base, $30-40.

#848 wide cupped tulip bowl, $150-175; #1522 10" crimped bowl, $175-200. *Courtesy of Fenton Museum.*

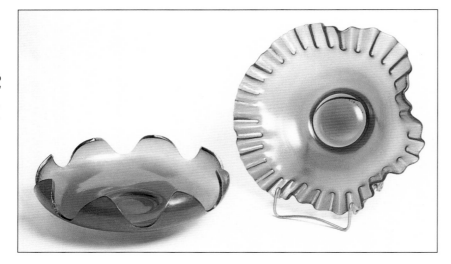

#156 14" banana boat (this is the only one the author has seen), $350+. *Courtesy of Phil & Nancy Waln.*

Possibly the #612 vase flared, crimped Jack in the Pulpit (rare shape), $200-250. Possibly the #1522 10" bowl in the banana bowl shape, $225-275.

#1623 dolphin Spiral Optic candles, $200-250 pr.; #1602 crimped bowl, $400-450.

#260 7" comport, $125-150; #847 rose bowl, $150-175; 6" comport (appears to be the same mold as the Iris Carnival glass comport), $150-200.

#556 cigarette holder, $200-250; #401 night set or tumble up, $175-225; #60 bath salts jar, $300-400. *Courtesy of Fenton Museum.*

#55 cologne with decoration, $225-275; #55 cologne with decoration, $225-275; mini puff box, $175-225; #59 cologne, $225-275. (Plastic or celluloid tray is not Fenton.) *Courtesy of Janet R. Reichling*

#56 cologne, $250-300; #60 bath salts jar, $300-400; #55 cologne, $225-275; #55 cologne with flat stopper, $225-275.

#55 1/2 flower final colognes: Wisteria Stretch, $500+; Tangerine Stretch, Price Und. (only one known); Celeste Blue Stretch, $400+. *Courtesy of Dave & Linda Rash.*

Toothpick holder, 2 5/8", $275-350; #923 individual nut cup, $50-75; (small) puff box, 3 1/4", $175-225; #57 puff box, 4 1/8" high, $150-175.

#222 pitcher with cutting, $600-700; #222 lemonade with handles, $125-150 ea. *Courtesy of Fenton Museum.*

#918 standard compote, 12" high, $350-450.

Chapter 4
Candlesticks: Stretch, Opaque, and Clear

Note: Prices for two-toned Stretch and Opaque candlesticks have escalated in the last few years. The method for pricing is that a single candlestick is worth forty percent of a pair. All prices listed here are for pairs.

#749 12" pair of Jade candles. Only pair known. Price Und. The only colors that the 12" candles are known in are Jade & Grecian Gold.

#349 10" candles: Ruby with cut ovals, $350-400; Chinese Yellow with cut ovals, $500-650; Pekin Blue, $300-400; Persian Pearl Stretch with cut ovals, $400-500. *Courtesy of Chester & Debby Moody.*

#249 6 1/2" candles: San Toy, $95-110; Florentine Green Stretch, $95-110; Celeste Blue Stretch, $75-95; Persian Pearl Stretch, $85-100; Ruby, $75-90. *Courtesy of Chester & Debby Moody.*

#649 10" candles: Topaz Stretch and Black, $400-500; #549 8" Topaz Stretch and Black, $300-350; #549 8" Moonstone and Black, $400+; #649 Flame & Cobalt Blue, $550+.

#649 12" candles: Jade, Price Und.; #549 8" Chinese Yellow with enameled decoration, $400+; #649 Chinese Yellow and black, $400+; #749 12" Grecian Gold, Price Und.

#649 Grecian Gold and black, $250-300; #549 Persian Pearl with threading, $300-350; #549 Chinese Yellow with enameled decoration, $400+; #549 Wisteria Stretch, $250-325; #649 10" Chinese Yellow and black, $400+.

#549 8" Mongolian Green with enameled decoration, $550+; #649 10" Mustard and black, $500+; #549 8" Grecian Gold and Persian Pearl, $300-350; #549 8" Wisteria and Persian Pearl, $350-400. *Courtesy of Chester & Debby Moody.*

#232 ribbed candles: Jade, $200-225; Grecian Gold, $175-200; Celeste, $175-200; Topaz, $175-200; Florentine, $175-200.

#349 10" Ruby with cut ovals,
$500-650; #449 8 1/2" Persian
Pearl, $300-350; #349 10"
Wisteria, $550-650; #349 10"
Florentine Green, $275-325.

#649 Mandarin Red, $275-325; #549 Flame, $350-400;
#549 Ruby, $200-225; #649 Black, $200-225.

#649 10" Chinese Yellow and
black, $400+; #549 Celeste and
Topaz Stretch, $275-350.

#549 8 1/2" Topaz Stretch, $200-250; #649 Wisteria & Persian Pearl Stretch. $400-475. *Courtesy of Fenton Museum.*

#649 10" Moonstone and black, $350-450; #549 Jade and Moonstone, $300-350. *Courtesy of Fenton Museum.*

#232 ribbed candles: Ruby, $200-225; Velva Stretch, $200-225; Wisteria Stretch, $300-350; Jade, $200-225; Cameo Opalescent, $225-250.

Wisteria Stretch candles: #649 10", $375-425; #232 8", $300-350; #249 6 1/2", $175-225; #449 8" cut ovals, $400-450; and #349 10", $300-350.

#449 8 1/2" Tangerine Stretch. Price Und. A pair of these was found in 2004. They are the first tall pair of Tangerine candlesticks that have turned up. *Courtesy of Gordon & Sue Phifer.*

#449 8 1/2" Ruby Stretch candles. Plain, $800-1000; cut ovals, Price Und.

#549 8" candles: Topaz and black, $225-300; Wisteria Stretch, $250-325; Celeste and black, $225-300.

#649 10" Mandarin Red; #549 8 1/2" Mandarin Red; #449 8 1/2" Mandarin Red candlesticks, $175-200 a pair; #549 8 1/2" Jade-Moonstone, $275-325 a pair; #649 10" Moonstone-Black, $275-325 a pair. *Courtesy of David & Linda Rash*

Chapter 5
Freehand Art Glass

Antique Blue/Green

#3014 4" Antique Blue vase with Karnak Hanging Vines, $1800+.

#3024 14" Egyptian vase in Antique Blue with medium blue tulips & stems. One known. $4500+.

#3056 12" Antique Blue Hanging Heart vase. Rare Shape. $2500+.

#3000 14" Antique Blue Hanging Heart vase, $2000+.

#3024 14" Antique Blue Hanging Heart vase, $2000+.

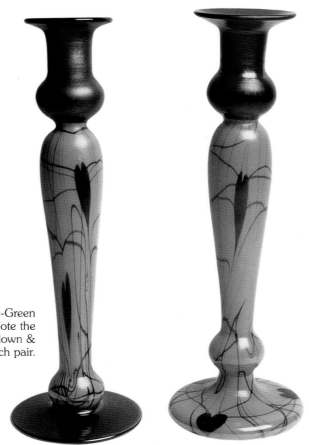

#3018 12" Antique Blue-Green Hanging Heart candlesticks. Note the two different bottoms: blown & attached. $2500+ for each pair.

91

#3004 9" Antique Blue Hanging Vine two-handled vase, $2000+.

Antique Blue candle with cobalt foot & top (whimsy), 9 1/2" tall, Price Und.
#3016 9 1/2" Antique Green Pulled Feather footed bowl with cobalt edge, $3000+. *Courtesy of Fenton Museum.*

#3026 11" Antique Blue Hanging Vine compote with cobalt foot. This is the rare large size. $3000+. The 9" size is usually seen.

#3018 12" candlesticks. Possibly white Hanging Heart, $2500+ pair. Antique Green Pulled Feather, $2500+ pair. *Courtesy of Fenton Museum.*

#3045 14" Antique Blue Hanging Vine vase, $2500+.

#3008 11" Antique Blue Hanging Vine vase, $2000+. *Courtesy of Jim & Sue Stage.*

#3040 puff boxes in Antique Green Hanging Hearts & Mosaic. Hanging Hearts, $1500+; Mosaic, $1200+.

Antique Green Hanging Heart 8" vase, $2000+; #3003 Antique Blue Hanging Vine footed 6" vase, $1500+.

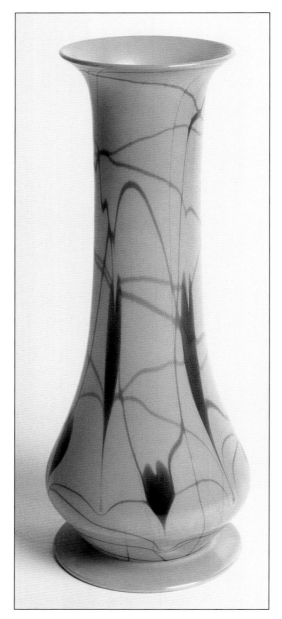

#3004 10 1/2" Antique Green vase with cobalt handles & threading. Price Und. *Courtesy of Fenton Museum.*

#3045 14" Antique Blue Hanging Heart vase, $2000+. *Courtesy of Fenton Museum.*

#3026 Antique Green Hanging Heart 9" bowl with cobalt foot, $2000+.

#3026 Antique Green Hanging Heart 9" comport, $2000+; Rare 11" Antique Blue Hanging Vine comport, $3000+.

#3026 Antique Green Hanging Heart 9" comport, $2000+; Antique Green Hanging Heart comport on an Opalescent Rib Optic base with cobalt connectors is very unique. Price Und.

Antique Green Hanging Heart 8" bowl on Opalescent Rib Optic foot. Price Und. (This was made for an uncle of Frank & Bill Fenton. It is one of best freehand pieces to be seen.)

Rare 7" Antique Green Pulled Feather vase with three ball feet. Price Und.

#3005 6 1/2" Antique Green Hanging Heart vase, $1200+.

#3039 6" Antique Green Pulled Feather
three-footed vase, $2500+.

Possibly #3016 10" Antique Green Hanging Heart bowl
with cobalt foot, $1800+. *Courtesy of Jim & Sue Stage.*

Possibly #3017 10" Antique Green Hanging Heart flat rolled bowl, $2000+.
Courtesy of Ed & Lori Radcliff.

#3013 6" Antique Green Hanging
Heart vase, $1700+.

#3018 12" Antique Green
Hanging Heart candles,
$3000+ pair. *Courtesy of Ed
& Lori Radcliff.*

#3036 Antique Green Hanging Heart 4" puff jar, $1500; 3" puff
jar, model # unknown, $1500+. *Courtesy of Ed & Lori Radcliff.*

#3028 8" Antique Green Hanging Heart fan vase, $1500+;
unlisted 7" pitcher, possibly from the #3004 vase mold, Price Und.

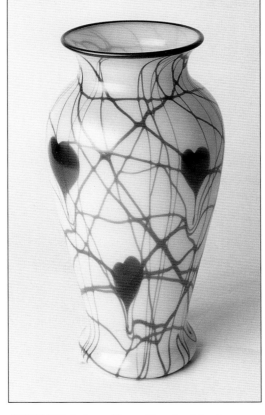

#3007 10" Antique Green Hanging Hearts vase,
$1800+. *Courtesy of Charles Griggs.*

Possibly #3033 14" Antique
Blue-Green Hanging Hearts
vase. (Rare shape.) $2250+.
Courtesy of Ed & Lori Radcliff.

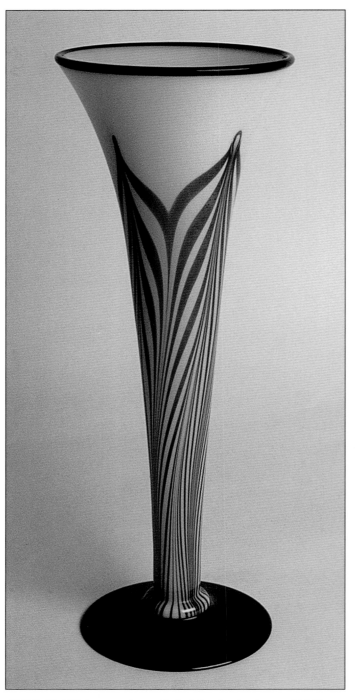

#3001 6" Antique Green Hanging Heart squat vase, $1800+.

#3020 12 1/2" Antique Green Pulled Feather bud vase, $1500+.

#3009 11" Hanging Heart handled vase, $2000+.

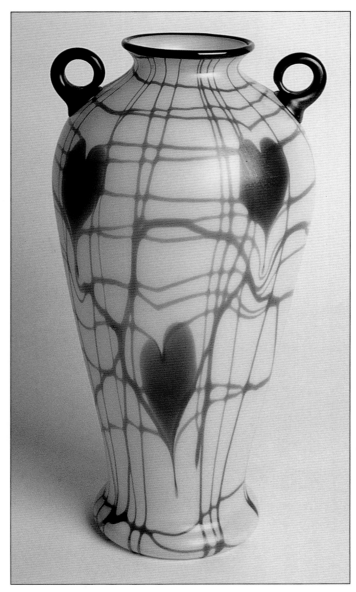

Karnak Red

This is the Rolls Royce of Fenton Art Glass. Pieces usually change hands privately. In the summer of 2004, there were two nice pieces on Ebay. One sold for $2800 and the other did not meet the reserve of $3000. In this author's opinion, if you can buy a good piece, with the exception of a bud vase, for approximately $3000 – do it. The values will only increase.

#3046 11" footed urn, $4000+; 10 1/2" Bulbous Rolled Rim vase, $4000+ (possibly made from the #3024 Egyptian vase). *Courtesy of Fenton Museum.*

#3013 6" vase with tulips, $3000+; #3004 10" Hanging Vine vase with cobalt handles, $3000+.

#3028 8" trumpet vase with cobalt spider web type decoration. (One known.) Price Und. *Courtesy of Fenton Museum.*

Hanging Vine 18" & 21" vases. Prices Und. (These are on display in the front case of the Fenton Museum. They had been in the Fenton family home for thirty-five years. It was the author's privilege to be allowed to photograph these pieces.)

#3035 High Footed bonbon, $4500+. Unlisted Karnak atomizer perfume. (Purchased from a 1920-'30s Fenton worker's estate.) Price Und. *Courtesy of Fenton Museum.*

#3006 10 1/2" vase with white tulips, $4000+; #3007 9" Hanging Heart vase, $3750+. *Courtesy of Fenton Museum.*

Unknown 5" Karnak vase with white tulips, $3000+. (Possibly the #3030 vase only with a foot in Antique Blue with Karnak tulips. Price unknown, but easily a minimum of $5000.)

#3039 6" three-footed Hanging Vine vase, $3500+; #3004 9" Hanging Vine vase, $3000+.

#3026 9" Hanging Vine footed bowl, $3500+.

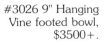

#3006 11" Hanging Vine vase, $3500+; #3046
11" Hanging Vine footed urn, $4000+.

#3006 10 1/2" vase with Karnak handles, $3500+; #3009 10"
Mosaic vase (rare shape), $2250+.

#3002 6 1/2" Hanging Vine vase, $3000+;
#3024 8" Hanging Vine vase, $3000+.

#3024 12" vase with silver hearts
& whimsy top, $5000+.

#3024 15" vase (plain). Rare with no decoration. (This picture does not do justice to the cherry red iridescence.) $3750+.

#3024 15" Fenton vase with cobalt foot, $3750+; #3024 12" vase with silver hearts, $5000+.

#3026 9" Hanging Hearts footed bowl, $3500+.

#3035 Hanging Vine high-footed bonbon, $4500+.

#3025 (rare) 7 1/2" Hanging Vine covered bowl, $5000+.

#3035 High Footed bonbon, $4500+; #3025 covered bowl, $5000+.

#3060 (rare) Hanging Vine tobacco jar with metal lid. Price Und.

#3060 Tobacco jar, Price Und.; #3025 covered bowl, $5000+.

#3010 7" Hanging Vine handled vase, $3500+.

103

#3013 6" Hanging Vine vase, $3000+.

Hanging Heart 8" vase. (Rare shape.) $3750+.
Courtesy of Jim & Sue Stage.

#3018 (Pair) 12" Hanging Vine candles
with cobalt top & feet, $4500+.

#3018 12" candlestick. All Karnak with silver
hearts. Pair, $4000+. *Courtesy of Charles Griggs.*

#3024 15" Hanging Heart vase,
$4000+.

#3024 vases 12", $4000+; 9", $3700+; and 15", $4500+. (Amazing Trio!)

#3024 6" Mosaic vase, $1200+; #3024 9" Karnak Hanging Heart
vase, $3700+.

Possibly #3004 9" Karnak Hanging Vine vase with cobalt applied
snake. (Rare.) Price Und. *Courtesy of Dave & Linda Rash.*

105

#3016 10" Karnak Hanging Vine footed bowl, $2750+.

#3030 12" Karnak Hanging Vine vase, $4500+.

Karnak 8" vase with tulip, $4000+.

#3007 9 1/2" Karnak (plain) vase, $2500+.

#3003 6 1/2" footed vase. Rare Mosaic on white. One known. Price Und. *Courtesy of Fenton Museum.*

#3055 7" footed oval comport on green. Price Und. *Courtesy of Fenton Museum.*

#3028 8" fan vase with a very rare fan vase flower block. Vase, $1500+; block, Price Und. *Courtesy of Harry Rosenthal, Jr.*

#3028 8" fan vase, $1500+; #3039 6" footed vase, $2000+.

#3004 9" vase, $2000+.

#3051 (rare) 10 1/2" vase, $2250+;
#3006 10 1/2" vase, $1700+.

#3027 candle chamber stick showing detail of original label. $600+ each.

Possibly a variation of the #3008 11" vase (unusual shape), $1400+. Unlisted 4 1/2" ivy or witches ball with chain. (This would hang in the doorway and guests would tap it upon entering the house.) From a boarding house who rented to Fenton workers in the 1920s. Price Und.

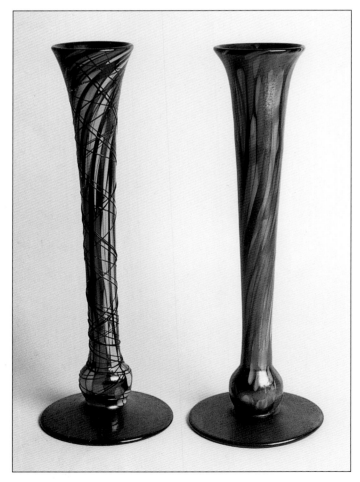

#3020 12" bud vases. Threaded, $1000+; not threaded, $800+.

Possibly #3008 11" vase, $1400+.

#3026 10" footed bowl, $2000+.

#3025 Mosaic covered bowl, $4000+.

Unknown 5" ivy ball or rose bowl, $1000+;
#3025 bonbon without lid, $1500+.

#3042 perfume with stopper out, $4000+.

#3042 perfume,
$4000+.

#3041 puff box, $1200+; #3042 (rare) bud vase variant made into cologne with stopper, $4000+.

#3043 6" wall vase, $800+.
Courtesy of Ed & Lori Radcliff.

#3055 7" footed oval comport, $1800+.

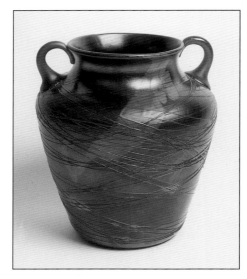

#3006 6 1/2" handled vase with unusual colors, $1800+.

#3000 11" vase, $2250+.

Variation of #3022 11" vase. (Rare shape.) $2500+. #3039 6" footed vase, $2000+.

Miscellaneous

#3020 12" bud vases: Antique Green with Hanging Hearts, $1250+; possibly jade green with Hanging Hearts, $1600+.

#3020 Antique Green bud vase, $1250+; #3020 jade green Jack in the Pulpit vase. (This was originally purchased from a family who's relative worked at Fenton factory in the 1920s.) Possibly one of a kind. Price Und.

#3003 6" jade green vase, $2000+.
Courtesy of Jim & Sue Stage.

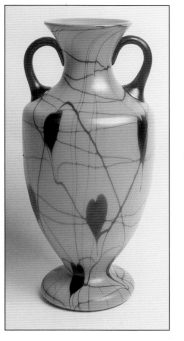

#3024 variant with blown foot of 12" vase in jade green with cobalt handles, $3000+.

#3040 6" Jade (blue/green) puff box (large size), $1700+.

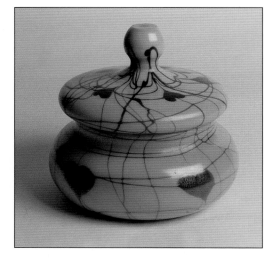

Unknown shape 6" in white with light blue Hanging Hearts and cobalt crest. Price Und.

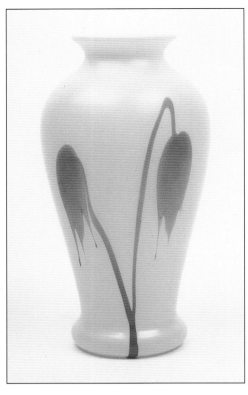

#3007 (rare) 9 1/2" vase in antique ivory or custard with Karnak tulips. Price Und.

#3053 (rare) 10" three-footed vase in lilac with dark amethyst hearts. Price Und. *Courtesy of Fenton Museum.*

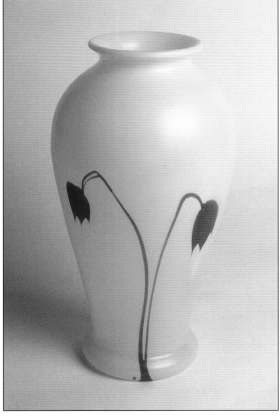

#3007 9" custard or ivory vase with Karnak tulips. Price Und.

Chapter 6
Special, Experimental Treatments and Decorations

Possibly #601 Sung Ko 10" shallow cupped bowl. Only one known. $600+.

#893 Sung Ko type three piece ginger jar, $1250+; #1934 8" vase, $600+. *Courtesy of Fenton Museum.*

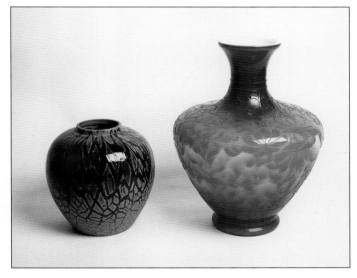

#898 Periwinkle Blue ginger jar with crackle type decoration, Price Und.; #898 vase with cameo type flowered cutting, Price Und. *Courtesy of Fenton Museum.*

#200 Sung Ko 5" rolled rim vase, $500+; #898 11" vase, $900+. *Courtesy of Jim & Sue Stage.*

#600 series Florentine Green flared bowl; #894 Chinese Yellow vase with frost type etch decorations. Prices Und. *Courtesy of Fenton Museum.*

#3 creamer & sugar, $400+; #847 cupped bowl in rare Lilac & Moonstone combination, $200+. *Courtesy of Fenton Museum.*

#1562 13" Chinese Yellow or mustard color canoe with black Oriental type decoration. Price Und. *Courtesy of Fenton Museum.*

#621 Moonstone vase with Oriental scene on black five-toed base. Base, $75-100. Vase, $300-400. (Otto Gertler decorated these Oriental scene vases.) *Courtesy of Fenton Museum.*

#621 6" Mandarin Red vase, $100-150 ea.; #846 6" cupped bowl on five-toed black bases. Gold leaf decorations. Bases, $75-200 ea. Bowl, $100-150. *Courtesy of Jim & Sue Stage.*

#318 candle, $60-75; #950 bowl, $150-175; #847 bowl in Mandarin Red with gold leaf decorations, $100-125. *Courtesy of Chester & Debby Moody.*

#893 Jade ginger jar with Oriental flower scene. One known. $600+. #846 Chinese Yellow bowl with dragon on five-toed base, $300-400. *Courtesy of Chester & Debby Moody.*

#893 Moonstone ginger jar with dragon decoration, $500+; #621 Pekin Blue 6 1/2" flared vase with dragon decoration, $400-500. *Courtesy of Randy & Debbie Coe.*

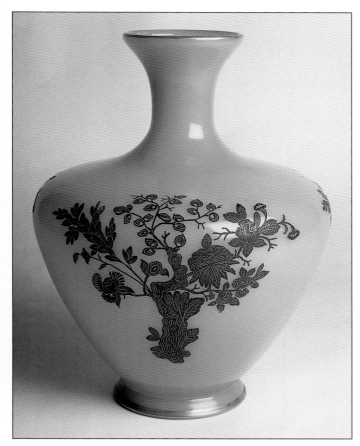

#898 11" vase with Oriental flower scene, $650+. One known.

#893 Chinese Yellow ginger jar with dragon, $600+; #621 Jade vase with dragon on five-toed base, vase, $300-400. *Courtesy of Jim & Sue Stage.*

#891 12" Jade vase, two known, $500+; #893 ginger jar with Oriental flower decoration, $600+. *Courtesy of Chester & Debby Moody.*

115

#893 Mandarin Red ginger jar with gold dragon & Oriental decoration. One known. $1500+.

Possibly #621 Crystal vase with tulip decoration. $125+.

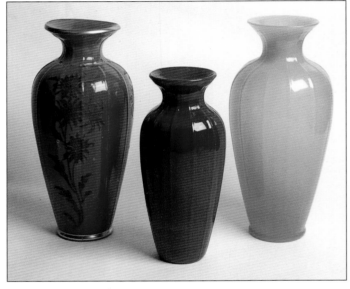

#891 12" Mandarin Red vase with flower decoration, $500+; #888 8" Mandarin Red vase, rare size (only six known), $500+; #891 12" Jade vase, $500+ (two known). *Courtesy of Chester & Debby Moody.*

Rose 9" fan vase with gold etched *Spirit of St. Louis*. Possibly Fenton. Three known. (Author has seen a black one with a gold plane. It sold on Ebay a couple years ago for $285.) *Courtesy of Keith C. Smith.*

#901 Chinese Yellow Dancing Ladies 5" urn, $300-325 (no lid); #893 ginger jar with dragon, $600+; 6" jug, $300-400. *Courtesy of Jim & Sue Stage.*

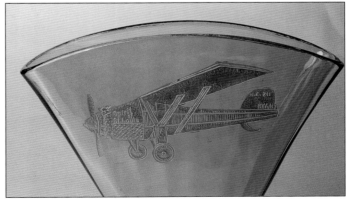

Detail of plane in the 9" rose fan vase.

Chapter 7

Figurals, Animals, Novelties, Non-Stretch, Non-Carnival

#1564 Orchid turtle flower block, $125-150; #1565 Green turtle with flower block insert, $150+; #1564 Celeste Blue turtle flower block, $125-150. Fenton turtles have six holes and Northwood models have eight holes.

#1565 Green turtle with #1538 Green Opalescent Button & Braids aquarium, $1400. *Courtesy of Carolyn & Woody Kriner.*

#1565 Black turtle, $300-350*. (Rare, two or three known.) *With #1538 Crystal Bubble Optic aquarium, $400+.

#1565 Green turtle with flower block insert, $500+. (The flower block inserts are extremely hard to find.)

#1565 Crystal turtle with flower block insert, $225-250. *Courtesy of Richard & Sara Speaight.*

#1565 turtle shown with block out.

#1565 Amber turtle, three known, $225-275; #1565 Crystal turtle, $200-250. *Courtesy of Richard & Sara Speaight.*

#1565 Crystal turtle & flower block insert, $225-275; #1618 elephant planter, scarce in crystal, $300-400. *Courtesy of Richard & Sara Speaight.*

#4 flower blocks (rare size). Rose, Moonstone, Jade, $75-100 ea.

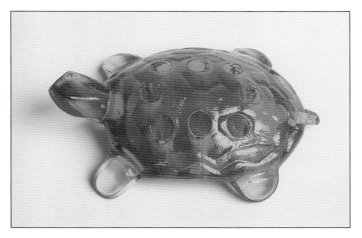

#1564 Tangerine turtle flower block, $250+. Only one known.

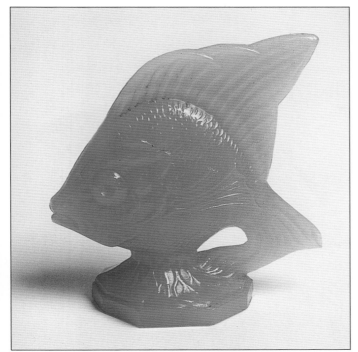

#306 Jade fish novelty, $100-125.

#1618 Celeste Blue elephant planter, $600+; #1618 Black Satin elephant planter, $1,000+. (Note: This Black planter was purchased from the late Bill Heacock in a parking lot at one of the Fenton conventions.)

#1502 Orchid diamond optic fan dolphin vase, $75-100; #1618 Orchid elephant planter, $500+.

#1618 Jade elephant planter, $700+. *Courtesy of Fenton Museum.*

#711 peacock bookends. Also known in pink satin. Pairs in satin colors, $550+; crystal, $400+. *Courtesy of Gordon & Sue Phifer.*

Detail of peacock bookend. *Courtesy of Fenton Museum.*

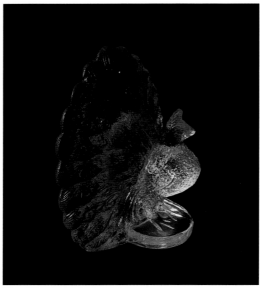

French Opalescent peacock bookend. One known. Price Und. A pair might easily sell for $500+.

Elephant whiskey bottles. Black, one known, Price Und. *Courtesy of Avril Ash.* Sheffield Blue, $500+. *Courtesy of Alexander Ash.* Periwinkle blue, one known, Price Und. *Courtesy of Fenton Museum.*

#307 Bulldog novelties: Jade, Ruby, Green, $50-90 ea. *Courtesy of Fenton Museum.*

#1645 September Morn nymphs & frogs. Jade, $250-300; Moonstone, $500-600; Chinese Yellow, $500-600; Pekin Blue, $600-700. *Courtesy of Dave & Linda Rash.*

#1645 Nymph & frog. $2000-3000. *Courtesy of John & Ann Fenton.*

#1645 Lilac nymph & frog in #848 cupped bowl. Only six of these have been seen. (Three sets have been sold at auction and Ebay for over $3000 each set). Estimate value for this set, $2000-3000. *Courtesy of John & Ann Fenton.*

#1645 Aquamarine nymph & frog, $400-500; #1502A bowl, $65-95. *Courtesy of John & Ann Fenton.*

#1645 Mandarin Red September Morn nymph, block bowl. Only a few true Mandarin Red nymphs are known. Nymph frog, $750+; bowl, $75-85. *Courtesy of Jim & Sue Stage.*

#1645 Custard nymph/frog. Appears to be milk glass but it glows under a black light – one known. Price Und. Crystal nymph in a Lucite type block. Sold as a perfume. Price Und.

Canoe ashtrays. Amber, Stretch, green, crystal, emerald, rose. Also known in aquamarine & other transparent colors. $30-40 ea. *Courtesy of Mike Soper.*

#1564 rose turtle flower block, $100-150; rose dolphin nut cup novelty, $150-175; #16 rose San Toy bath jar, $100-150. (I have recently been advised the noniridized, i.e. pink/crystal combinations might not be Fenton.) *Courtesy of Fenton Museum.*

Rose/crystal dolphin nut cup novelty, $150-175.

Shell 2" ashtrays. Cobalt, emerald, milk, black, ruby, rose, Sheffield Blue, orchid, jade, $20-40 each. 4 1/2" ruby shell with advertisement, $40-50. *Courtesy of Gordon & Sue Phifer.*

Chapter 8
Opaque

Chinese Yellow

#1504A Chinese Yellow dolphin bowl on black five-toed base. Base, $75-100; Bowl, $150-175. *Courtesy of Chester & Debby Moody.*

#543 Chinese Yellow flat bonbon, $150-175.

Chinese Yellow 6" jug. $275-350.

#900 Chinese Yellow Dancing Ladies bowl, $300-400; #1681 Chinese Yellow Big Cookies jar with lid, $325-400.

#8 1/2 lb. Chinese Yellow candy, $100-150; #1668 8" flip vase, $225-275. *Courtesy of Dave & Linda Rash.*

#314 Chinese Yellow candle, $75-125 pr.; #315 Chinese Yellow candle, $75-100 pr.;
#318 Chinese Yellow candle, $75-100 pr. *Courtesy of Dave & Linda Rash.*

#1663 oval 11" bowl, $150-175; #857 8" fan vase, $95-100.

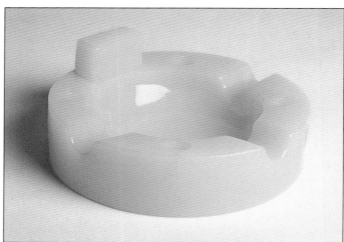

#202 ashtray. (This is the first opaque the author has seen.
Usually found in Stretch.) $175-225. *Courtesy of Wayne &
Beverly McKeenan.*

Chinese Yellow 14" lamp vase. (Usually seen in Mandarin
Red. Three known in Jade.) $350+. #1639 (rare)
Elizabeth 8" plate, $65+.

Black

#1790 Black Leaf Tiers flared bowl. $175-250.

#1564 5 1/2" Black Square planter. One known.
$100-125. *Courtesy of Thomas K. Smith.*

Jade

#1635 Jade pitcher, $250-300.

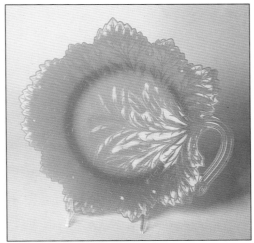

#175 11" leaf cake plate. Few known in this
size. $125-175. *Courtesy of Ed & Pat Anderson.*

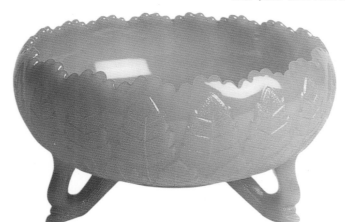

#1790 10" cupped Leaf
Tiers bowl. $225-275.

#100 Jade tumbler, $30-40. Pitcher, $175-225. Creamer & sugar, $70-90 pr.

#844 Jade flower finial candy, $225-275.
Courtesy of Dave & Linda Rash.

#1124 Jade Butterfly & Berry hatpin holder. One known. Price Und.

#918 Jade 12" high standard compote, $150-200.

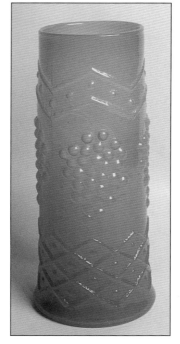

#1563 Jade Lattice & Grape vase. One known. Price Und.

#10 Jade candy, three known, $225-275; #1564 Jade square planter, one known, $200-275; #1124 Jade Butterfly & Berry hatpin holder, Price Und.

#59 Jade cologne, $150-200; #56 Jade cologne, $175-225; #16 Bath jars with gold decoration, $75-100 ea.

#1502 fan vase with Jade block. (This is the way it was purchased at the Fenton convention in 2000.) Vase, $60-75; block, Price Und.

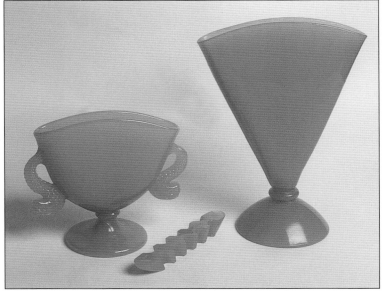

#1502 Jade dolphin fan vase, $45-55; 5 1/2" jade fan vase flower black, two known, Price Und.; #562 Jade fan vase, $55-65.

#1502 cupped dolphin bowl with gold dolphins, $100-150; #680 plate with Yellow Crest, four known, Price Und.; #894 10" vase with etched flowers, $175-250. *Jade cupped bowl with pheasant etch on black five-toed base. Base, $75-100. Bowl, $125-150.

#600 8" bowl and #621 6" cupped vase with flower band decoration. $85-110 ea.

Jade 8" strawberry jar. (One known.) Price Und. *Courtesy of Fenton Museum.*

Jade shaving mug, $70-90; #1639 syrup pitcher with lid, $150-200. *Courtesy of Fenton Museum.*

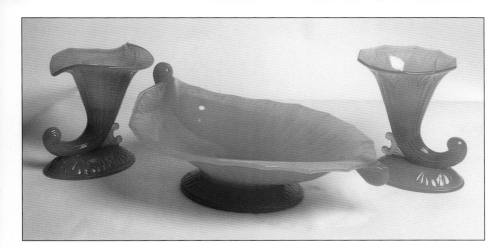

#950 cornucopia console
set bowl, $120-150.
Candles, $120-160 pr.

#1663 oval bowl & plate. (This is the first
plate the author had seen made out of the
bowl in any color.) Jade bowl, $125-150.
Plate, $150-225.

Lilac

#1536 Lilac comport, $135-165; #1639 Lilac syrup pitcher with
lid, $175-325; #1681 Lilac Big Cookies jar with lid, $450-500.

#844 flower finial candy, one known, $750+;
#835 1/2 lb. candy jar, $175-250. *Courtesy of
Charles Griggs.*

#844 flower finial candy. $750+.

#1681 Lilac Big Cookies basket, $300-350; #1639 Lilac batter jug with lid, $300-400; #1533 Lilac flared compote, $125-150.

#1504A 9" cupped bowl, $150-225.

#2318 Lilac candelabras, $200-250 pr.

#1554 Lilac flowerpot & plate, $225-275; #1639 Lilac syrup pitcher with lid, $275-325.

#1502 oval bonbon. (Opaque is rare with diamond optic.) $225-300. *Courtesy of Nick Duncan.*

Flame and Mandarin Red

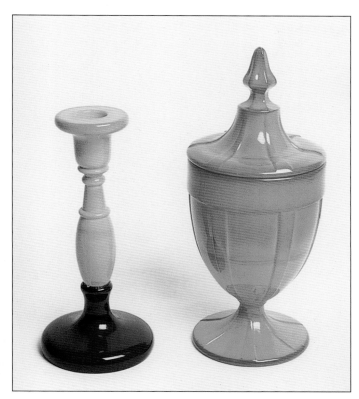

#847 6" fan vase. Unusual swirl colors. $125-150. *Courtesy of Jon & Bev Spencer.*

#549 Flame candlestick, $200-250 pr.; #636 Flame 1 lb. candy, $100-125. *Courtesy of Fenton Museum.*

#848 Petal candles, $175-225 pr. *Courtesy of Wayne & Beverly McKeehan.*

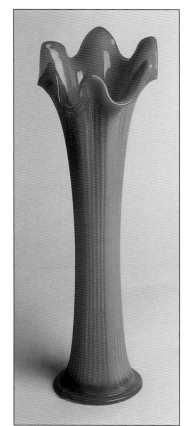

#180 Hyacinth vase, $200-300; #919 Mikado cake plate, $300-400. *Courtesy of Fenton Museum.*

Flame vase in the fine rib pattern, $150+.

#315 candlestick in Chinese Yellow, $150-200 pr.; Mandarin Red, $125-175 pr. *Courtesy* of *Chester & Debby Moody.*

#9 1/2 lb. candy, $125-150. (rare) 9" flared spittoon bowl on black five-toed base. Base: $75-100, bowl: one known, Price Und. #315 candlestick, $125-175 pr. *Courtesy of Chester & Debby Moody.*

#920 10" Grape & Cable bowl, $350-400; 12" bowl, $400-500.

#251 10" bud vase, $75-100; #1684 macaroon jar with lid, $175-225.

#893 ginger jar with flower cutting. Similar to the Ruby #184 12" vase. $325-375.

#920 12" cupped Grape & Cable bowl, $400-500; #1790 cupped Leaf Tiers bowl, $275-325. *Courtesy of Jim & Sue Stage.*

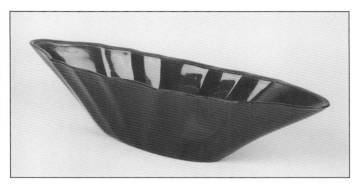

#1562 Mandarin Red canoe. One known. $200+.
Courtesy of Tim & Kathy Eicholz.

#736 1 lb. Mandarin Red covered candy, $150-200; #1503 spiral optic 10" bowl (optics are rare in opaque colors), $125-150.

#891 12" vase, $350-400; #888 8" vase, $500+. (Only four known. Mandarin Red is the only color that the 8" #888 vase has shown up in. If you find it in another color or treatment, please contact the author.) (See article "Fenton's Old 891" by Roy Ash, *Glass Collector's Digest,* April-May 1996) *Courtesy of Fenton Museum.*

#920 12" Grape & Cable bowl, $400-500; #919 Mikado comport, $250-350.
Courtesy of Jim & Sue Stage.

#898 11 1/2" Mandarin Red vase, $600-700.
Courtesy of Dave & Linda Rash.

#1934 vases in Sung Ko, $ 600+, and Mandarin Red, $350-450.

#621 vases – three sizes: 5" Wisteria Stretch, $90-100; 6" Mongolian Green, $60-70;
and 8" Mandarin Red diamond optic, $175-200. *Courtesy of Fenton Museum.*

#919 milk glass Mikado cake plate, $225-250.

#1563 milk glass Lattice & Grape vase, $150-175.

#920 10" Grape & Cable milk glass bowl, $125-150.

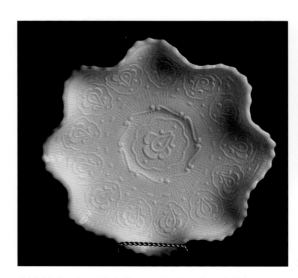

#1044 Persian Medallion milk glass bowl. (This is the first one the author has seen.) $75-100.

#950 Mongolian Green cornucopia console set. (Only two sets of candles known.) Bowl, $175-250; Candles, $275-350 pr. *Courtesy of Dave & Linda Rash.*

#893 Mongolian Green ginger jar, base, and lid, $350-450. *Courtesy of Jim & Sue Stage.*

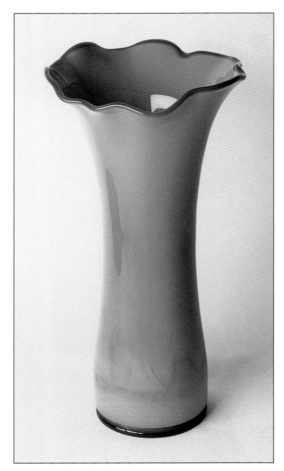

#304 Mongolian Green ashtray with flower, $75-85; #308 cigarette box, $250-300. *Courtesy of Dave & Linda Rash.*

Mongolian Green 12" swung vase. One known, $250+. *Courtesy of Charles Griggs.*

Moonstone

#2318 Moonstone candelabra, $150-200 pr.; #4 Moonstone flower block, Price Und. Also known in jade. #1608 Moonstone oval dolphin bowl, $275-325; #848 Moonstone candlestick, $100-150 pr.; #1645 September Morn nymph & frog, $600+.

#1681 Big Cookies basket, $250-325; #1608 oval dolphin bowl, $275-325; #2318 candelabra, $150-200 pr.

#893 ginger jar, base, and lid, $400-450; #846 cupped bowl, $65-86 (on black five-toed base, $75-100). *Courtesy of Fenton Museum.*

Mustard

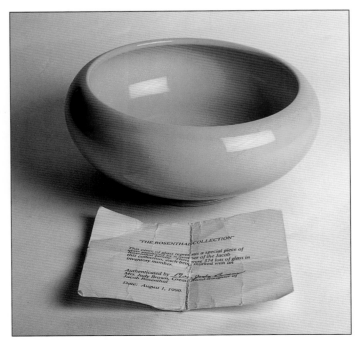

#601 Mustard 10" bowl. Certificate from the Rosenthal auction. $200-225.

137

Pekin Blue

#621 Pekin Blue 6" vase with Oriental decoration by Otto Gertler, $350-400; #1681 Pekin Blue Big Cookies basket, $275-325. *Courtesy of Dale & Eileen Robinson.*

#1608 Pekin Blue 10" oval footed bowl, $300-375. *Courtesy of Dave & Linda Rash.*

#1504A cupped bowl, $175-225 (five-toed black base, $75-100). *Courtesy of Charles Griggs.*

#9 3/4 lb. Pekin Blue covered candy, $100-150; 6" jug, $350-400; #249 6" candlestick, $125-175 pr. *Courtesy of Dave & Linda Rash.*

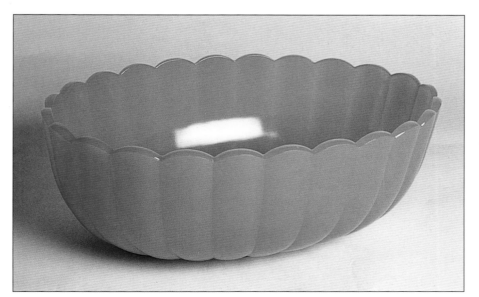

#1663 12" oval bowl. $175-225.

#1681 Big Cookies basket, $275-325; #848 Petal candle, $125-150 pr.; #1681 Moonstone Big Cookies basket, $250-325. *Courtesy of Chester & Debby Moody.*

#848 Petal candles. Kitchen Green (c. 1942 for Paul), $125-175 pr. Moonstone, $100-150 pr; Pekin Blue, $125-150 pr. *Courtesy of Chester & Debby Moody.*

#848 Kitchen Blue Petal candle. Only a few known. Bowl not seen. $125-175 pr.

Periwinkle Blue

#950 9" flat bowl, $150-200. (Note: The #950 candles are not known in Periwinkle. If you have a pair, please contact the author.) *Courtesy of Jim & Sue Stage.*

#1504A bottom of Periwinkle blue dolphin intaglio bowl, $350-450. *Courtesy of Dave & Linda Rash.*

#1933 rare 5" cupped bowl. One known, $125-175. *Courtesy of Dave & Linda Rash.*

Black five-toed base with original label, $100-125.

#1681 Big Cookies covered jar in an unusual butterscotch color. (This could be a bad batch of flame.) Price Und. *Courtesy of Melvin & Norma Lampton.*

Perfume Sets

#53 perfume, Lilac with Jade stopper, $200-225; #53 Lilac with Jade powder box, $175-200; #53 Moonstone perfume with jade stopper, $175-200. *Courtesy of Charles Griggs.*

#53 Jade with Lilac set on #1502 tray. $650-800 complete.

#16-17-54 Jade & Black bath set with flowered stoppers. $600+. (This set was donated to the Fenton Museum *in memory of Bill & Don Fenton* by the author.) *Courtesy of Fenton Museum.*

#53 Moonstone with Black set on tray. $600-750 complete.

#16 Chinese Yellow square bath jars with Pekin Blue and Moonstone stoppers, $150-175 ea.

Chapter 9
Dancing Ladies

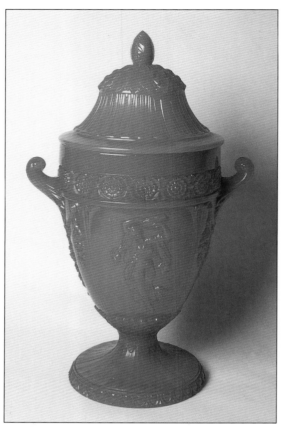

#901 18" covered urn, $3500+; #901 12"
Pekin Blue covered urn, $1750+.

#901 18" Dancing Ladies covered urn. (There are
four complete examples known. There is one with an
ebony lid and one without a lid.) $3500+ complete.

#901 5" covered urns. Pekin Blue, $700+; Moonstone, $500+; Jade, $600+;
Chinese Yellow, $1000+. *Courtesy of Dave & Linda Rash and Jim & Sue Stage.*

#901 12" Pekin Blue covered urn, $1750+ (two known); #901 Topaz Opalescent covered urn, $2000+. *Courtesy of Bill Crowl.*

#901 (rare) Ruby, no handle, covered urn, $1500+ (one known). *Courtesy of Dave & Linda Rash.*

#900 Cobalt Blue & transparent green bowls. (Only #900 known in cobalt. Usually but seldom found in #901 vases.) $700+ (only green one known); $600+. *Courtesy of Bill Crowl.*

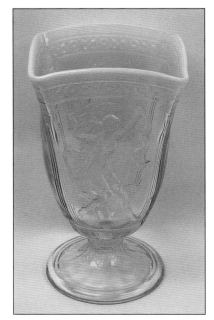

#901 French Opalescent square type vase, $600+.

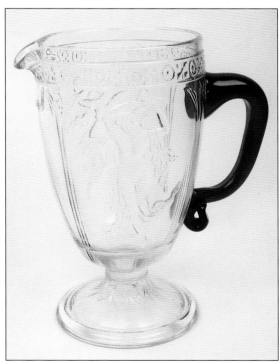

#901 Crystal vase made into a pitcher with an applied cobalt handle. (Only two known.) Price Und. *Courtesy of Bill Crowl.*

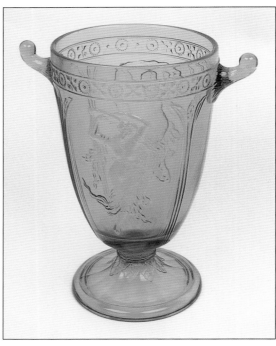

#901 5" Pekin Blue covered urn, $700+;
#900 11" Pekin Blue oval bowl, $400+.
Courtesy of Jim & Sue Stage.

#901 Mandarin Red vases. Flared, cupped, fan,
crimped. $750+ each. *Courtesy of Bill Crowl.*

#901 10" Amber urn – no lid. Price Und.
Courtesy of Bill Crowl. (A complete urn
with lid was recently found, $1200+.)

#901 9" Mandarin Red square top vase, $750+.

#901 Mandarin Red fan vase, $750+.

144

#901 Satin crimped vase, $300+. *Courtesy of Bill Crowl.*

#901 Topaz Opalescent flared cupped vase, $800+.
Courtesy of Dale & Eileen Robinson.

#901 Periwinkle Blue flared and chimney top vases,
$550+ ea. *Courtesy of Dave & Linda Rash.*

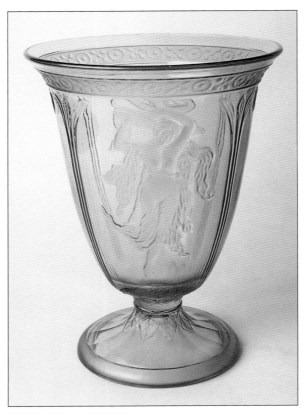

#901 Periwinkle Blue vase with an noncrimped top. (This is the first unfinished example the author has seen.) $500-600. *Courtesy of Nick Duncan.*

#901 Dancing Ladies vase in what appears to be Crystal Satin turned to sun purple. Price Und. *Courtesy of Charles Griggs.*

#901 Mongolian Green vases. Crimped, flared, chimney top. $500+ ea. *Courtesy of Dave & Linda Rash.*

Chapter 10
Patterns & Non-Opaque

Basket Weave

#1091 bowls: Mongolian Green, $175-200; Mandarin Red, $150-175.
Courtesy of Ed & Pat Anderson.

#1091 Mongolian Green Basket Weave bowls, $175-200; milk
glass (rare shape), $50-75; Mandarin Red, $150-175. *Courtesy of
Ed & Pat Anderson.*

Butterfly Net

Butterfly Net - Blue Opalescent
sherbet, $150-175; French Opalescent
tumbler, $200-225. Rare butterfly net
pieces. (This author has seen less than
ten pieces of this pattern. You are
fortunate if you own a piece.) *Courtesy
of Fenton Museum.*

Daisy & Button

#1900 Vaseline Daisy & Button Cape Cod 9 1/4" fan vase, $65-85.

#1900 Vaseline vanity set on #957 tray, $225-275. *Courtesy of Fenton Museum.*

#1900 10" Ruby Cape Cod vase, $75-125. *Courtesy of Charles Griggs.*

#1900 Cobalt vanity set on #957 tray, $200-250.

#1900 hand cornucopia vases. Colonial Blue, Vaseline, Wisteria, $45-65 ea.

#1620 Steigel green Plymouth ice tea, $40-50; 2 1/2 oz. flat whiskey, $35-40; #1900 Steigel green Daisy & Button sugar & creamer, $45-65; #1900 basket, $55-65.

Diamond Optic

#1502 flared dolphin compotes: Royal Blue, $125-175;
Ruby, $60-75. *Courtesy of Nick Duncan.*

Elizabeth

#1639 Elizabeth* pattern: Black batter jug and syrup pitcher on a
tray. Batter jug, $200-250; syrup, $125-175; tray, $50-75. (*Note:
Margaret & Kenn Whitmyer named this pattern in honor of
Elizabeth Fenton, the late wife of Mr. Frank M. Fenton.) *Courtesy
of Fenton Museum.*

#1639 footed two-tone ice teas. Jade/black foot, $35-45;
black/Moonstone foot (rare), $65-80; black/jade foot,
$35-45. *Courtesy of Fenton Museum.*

#1639 tumblers, sherbets, creamers, sugars. Black ice tea/Moonstone foot, $65-80.
Black sherbet/Moonstone foot, $50-65. Black ice tea/jade foot, $35-45. Jade/black
foot, flared sherbet (scarce shape), $35-45. Creamer & sugar, $85-125 pr.

#1639 Jade center handle server. The handles on these are the same as on the Lincoln Inn servers, $150-225. #1700 Jade Lincoln salt & pepper on rare black tray. Shakers, $250-300 pair; tray, Price Und. *Courtesy of Fenton Museum - loaned by Tom & Karin Sanders.*

Jade center handled server, $150-225. *Courtesy of Fenton Museum.*

Rare Pekin Blue/Moonstone powder jar, $250-325. *Courtesy of Fenton Museum.*

#1639 Jade/black footed powder box, $175-225. Covered mint jar, $150-200.

Black/jade creamer & sugar, $85-125 pr. Rare Moonstone with Ruby foot sherbet, $75-85. Jade/Moonstone ice tea, $60-75. Black/Moonstone sherbet, $50-65. *Courtesy of Gordon & Sue Phifer.*

Rare Ruby/cobalt pieces. (This author has only seen a handful of these in the past year.) Sherbet, $75-85. Ice teas, $85-100 ea. *Courtesy of Fenton Museum.*

Ruby/Cobalt, Cobalt/Ruby sherbets, $75-85 ea. *Courtesy of Fenton Museum.*

Cobalt 10" plate with etched border, $75-95. *Courtesy of Thomas K. Smith.*

All Ruby luncheon set (rare): ice teas, $45-50 ea.; plate, $25-35; sherbet, $35-40. *Courtesy of Thomas K. Smith.*

#1639 Royal Blue Elizabeth pieces with cuttings: Crystal foot iced tea, $50-60; 8 1/2" plate, $35-45; sherbet, $40-50. *Courtesy of Charles Griggs.*

Flowered Windows

This pattern was made for a brief time in 1938. The molds were turned out for hobnail and the rest is history. Plate and ice teas also made. Crystal sherbet, $15-20. Rare Colonial Blue water, $55-75; Ruby wines, $30-35.

Colonial Blue flowered windows ice tea, $65-85; wine, $55-65. (Colonial Blue is the hardest color to find in this pattern.)

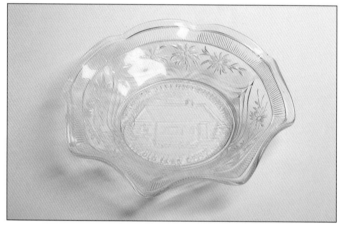

Crystal flowered windows showing stems. Ice tea, $25-35; water, $25-35; sherbet, $20-25; wine, $20-25.

Flowered windows 10" bowl with Marietta land office decoration, $75-125. *Courtesy of Fenton Museum.*

Franklin

#1935 6 1/2" Ruby (rare) Franklin tumbler (very few known), Price Und.; 2 1/2" Amber whiskey, $15-20 ea. *Courtesy of Gordon & Sue Phifer.*

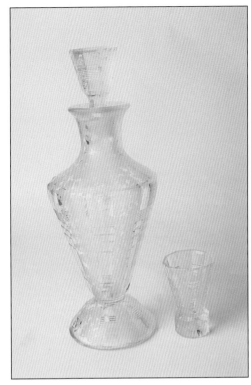

#1935 Ruby Franklin decanter, $200-125. Whiskey, $20-25 ea. *Courtesy of Dave & Linda Rash.*

#1935 Franklin decanter & whiskey with Ming etch. One known. Decanter, $150-175; whiskey, $25-35 ea. *Courtesy of Charles Griggs.*

Georgian

#1611 Georgian, rare Black pieces: water, $35-45; wine, $30-35, cupped compote, Price Und.; 1 oz. footed cordial, $25-35; juice tumbler, $20-30.

#1611 Black creamer & sugar, $75-100 pr.; 54 oz. jug, $150-200.

#1611 Black wine, $30-35; Black water, $35-45; Amber beer mug, $30-35; Crystal mug, $20-30. *Courtesy of Fenton Museum.*

#1611 Ruby compote, made from a water goblet, Price Und. Cobalt spittoon vase from a candy jar bottom, Price Und. Milk glass candle: ruby & cobalt pairs bring $65-85; milk glass would be slightly less.

Ruby compote from candy bottom, Price Und. Ruby covered candy, $100-125.

1 oz. footed cordials, $15-20 ea. Ruby decanter & stopper, $100-125. *Courtesy of Fenton Museum.*

Grape & Cable

#920 Grape & Cable 12" Cobalt Blue bowl (one known), $350+;
#920 10" Ruby bowl, $1000+. *Courtesy of Mike Soper.*

#920 Amethyst Grape & Cable bowl, $225-300; #349 Wisteria
cut oval candles, $300-400 pr. *Courtesy of Charles Griggs.*

Leaf Tiers

#1790 Leaf Tiers Cobalt
candle, $125-150 pr.; 10"
bowl, $150-175. *Courtesy
of Fenton Museum.*

#1790 Topaz Opales-
cent candle, $150-200
pr.; 10" bowl, $200-
250. These are the
only pieces I have seen
in this color. *Courtesy
of Fenton Museum.*

#1790 Transparent Green candles, $75-100. *Courtesy of Thomas K. Smith.*

#175 Cobalt 11" leaf plates. $125-150; 8" plates, $35-45. *Courtesy of Ed & Pat Anderson.*

#1790 Amethyst Leaf Tiers plate, $150-175.

#1790 Amber Leaf Tiers candles, $75-115 pr.

Lincoln Inn

Ruby & cobalt flared cocktails, $75-100 ea. Crystal example shown is not Fenton but a cut glass example. I am picturing it so you may see the difference in thickness. It is much lighter & thinner. Not priced. *Courtesy of Gordon & Sue Phifer.*

Top detail showing thickness of glass on flared cocktails. *Courtesy of Gordon & Sue Phifer.*

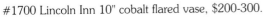

#1700 Lincoln Inn 10" cobalt flared vase, $200-300.

Orchid sherbet, $30-35. Ruby 10" square top vase, $175-225. Steigel green water goblet. This is the only piece that is known in this color. (Gift of the author to the Fenton Museum.) Price Und. Green Opalescent flared cocktail (three or four known), Price Und. *Courtesy of Fenton Museum.*

Shakers and black tray. Tray, Price Und. Shakers: Ruby, $200-250 pr.; Jade, $250-300 pr.; Black, $350-275 pr.; Crystal, $150-200 pr. I have also seen a single pink shaker. *Courtesy of Gordon & Sue Phifer.*

Green Opalescent flared cocktail. Price Und. Persian Pearl Stretch cup. (This is the only piece of iridized Lincoln Inn that has surfaced.) Price Und. *Courtesy of Fenton Museum – loaned by Les & Roxanne Rowe.*

Very possibly a pair of black candles. (Frank Fenton believes they are possibly made from a compote.) Price Und.

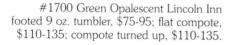

#1700 Green Opalescent Lincoln Inn footed 9 oz. tumbler, $75-95; flat compote, $110-135; compote turned up, $110-135.

#1700 Aquamarine Lincoln Inn cup & saucer, $35-45 set; gold sherbet, $35-45.

#1700 Jade Lincoln Inn set. (L-R: cocktail, $30-35; water, $40-45; sherbet, $30-35; dinner plate (rare), $70-90; lunch plate, $25-30; cup & saucer, $35-40 set.

#1700 Black sherbet, $55-65; ruffled compote, $75-85.

1700 Lincoln Inn bowls with intaglio fruit. 8", $45-60; 10", $60-90. *Courtesy of Fenton Museum.*

Peacock, Apple Tree and Other Vases

#791 Peacock vases: 10" flared French Opalescent, $250+; 8" emerald green (only one known), $250+; 6" flared cupped milk glass, $200+; 4" flared milk glass, $150+. (Note: Any sizes except 8" are hard to find.). *Courtesy of Mike Soper.*

Orange Tree 11" crimped bowl in an Aquamarine type color, $175-225. *Courtesy of Fenton Museum.*

#1602 10" footed crimped intaglio fruit dolphin bowl. Only a few known. Possibly Cape Cod green color. $200+. *Courtesy of Chester & Debby Moody.*

#1561 Emerald green Apple Tree vase, $250+ (two known); #791 Peacock vase in emerald green (one known), $250+. *Courtesy of Mike Soper.*

#1561 Emerald green Apple Tree vase, $250+; #1561 Jade Apple Tree vase, $250-275. *Courtesy of Mike Soper.*

#1562 10" Royal Blue blueberry vase (only a few known), $275+; #1561 Royal Blue Apple Tree vase, $250-275. *Courtesy of Mike Soper.*

#1561 Royal Blue Apple Tree vase, $250-175; powder blue Apple Tree vase actually c. 1942 for Edward P. Paul, $175-225. *Courtesy of Mike Soper.*

#1561 powder blue Apple Tree vase, $175-225; #1110 11" Milady vase (only a few known), $250-300. *Courtesy of Mike Soper.*

#1561 Satin Apple Tree vase, $175-200; #791 Satin Peacock vase, $175-200. *Courtesy of Mike Soper.*

161

#1561 French Opalescent Apple Tree vase, $200-225. Crystal tumbler, $20-30. Crystal Apple Tree vase, $125-175. *Courtesy of Mike Soper.*

#1561 Silver Crest Apple Tree vase. Very few known. $275-325. Milk glass tumbler, $30-40; Silver Crest Apple Tree pitcher (only three known), $300-400. *Courtesy of Mike Soper.*

#1563 Ruby Lattice & Grape vase (one known), $275-325; #1561 Ruby Apple Tree vase with chimney top, $200-225. *Courtesy of Mike Soper.*

#1561 Topaz Opalescent vase, $200-250. Rare Topaz Opalescent rib optic vase. Four known. $600+. *Courtesy of Mike Soper.*

#1561 Topaz Opalescent rib optic Apple Tree vase, $600+. *Courtesy of Mike Soper.*

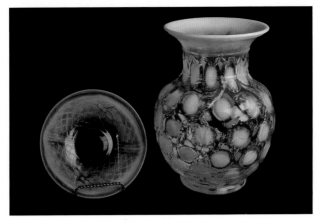

French Opalescent butterfly net 6" plate, $150-175;
#1561 French Opalescent dot optic Apple Tree vase.
One known. $300+.

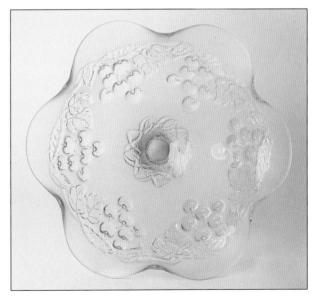

#919 Cherries compote. One known with
Cherries interior, $250+. *Courtesy of
Charles Griggs.*

#919 Royal Blue Mikado cake plate, $350-425. *Courtesy of Charles Griggs.*

Detail of Cherries compote.

#1110 Royal Blue Milady vase,
$300-350. *Courtesy of Charles
Griggs.*

#1110 Crystal Satin Ming
Milady vase, $175-250. *Courtesy
of Charles Griggs.*

#1620 Plymouth Royal Blue cocktail shaker, $200-250. *Courtesy of Roy D. Ash.*

Royal Blue ice teas, $35-45. Steigel green 2 1/2 oz. whiskey, $30-40. Royal Blue cocktail shaker, $200-250. *Courtesy of Fenton Museum.*

#1620 Plymouth Ruby cocktail shaker, $175-225. Amber cocktail shaker. This is the only one I have seen. $200-275. *Courtesy of Chester & Debby Moody.*

Ruby old fashioned, $30-40. Ruby bar bottle (rare), $275-325. (I know many people who have been searching for this for a long time.) Ruby pilsner, $40-50. *Courtesy of Gordon & Sue Phifer.*

#1620 Crystal Ming flat juice, $25-35. Crystal Ming cocktail shaker, $150-175. Crystal Ming old fashioned, $30-35. Crystal bar bottle, $175-225. Crystal 2 1/2 oz. whiskey, $20-25. *Courtesy of Gordon & Sue Phifer.*

Blue with satin tumbler, $60-70.
Steigel green old fashioned, $40-45.

#1620 Cobalt Plymouth: ice tea, $45-55; water, $45-50; wine, $40-45.

#1620 Blue water, $45-60. Blue with satin tumbler, $60-70. French Opalescent double pilsner, $75-95. French Opalescent mug, $75-95. French Opalescent 6" tumbler with cobalt handle, Price Und. *Courtesy of Fenton Museum.*

#1620 Plymouth Cobalt ice tea, $45-55; Steigel Green flat water, $35-45; Amber flat juice, $25-30; Ruby whiskey, $30-35.

#1934 decanters & wines. Ruby with platinum rings, $125-175; French Opalescent rib optic, $175-200; Royal Blue with rings, $125-175; amber with rings, $125-150; wines, $15-25 ea. *Courtesy of Chester & Debby Moody.*

#184 San Toy amber vase, $85-100; #1681 amber Big Cookies covered jar, $175-225.

Sheffield

#950 Sheffield Blue Silver Tone candle, $45 ea.; #1800 Sheffield Blue candle, $40 ea.

166

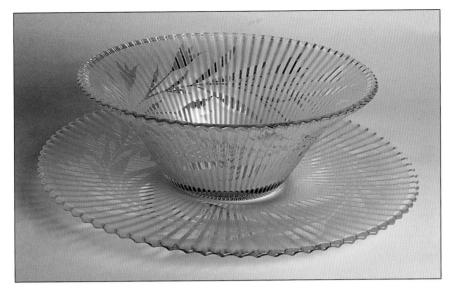

#1800 Blue Sheffield Silver Tone 12" bowl, $75-100; 14" under plate, $75-95. *Courtesy of Melvin & Norma Lampton.*

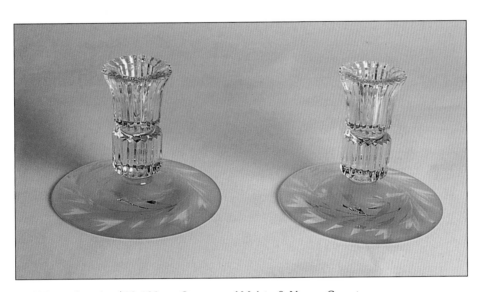

#1800 candlesticks, $90-100 pr. *Courtesy of Melvin & Norma Campton.*

#1800 Sheffield Blue rose bowl, $25-35; #1800 Sheffield Blue Silver Tone 10" vase, $75-95.

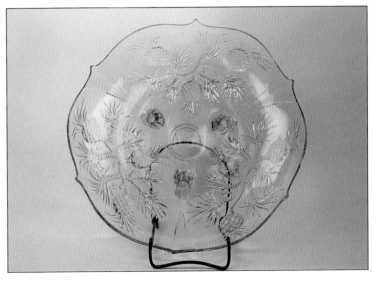

#1000 Sheffield Blue pineapple bowl, $80-100.

Miscellaneous

Amethyst Opalescent Stagg & Holly crimped bowl. (Three known.) $300+. *Courtesy of Fenton Museum.*

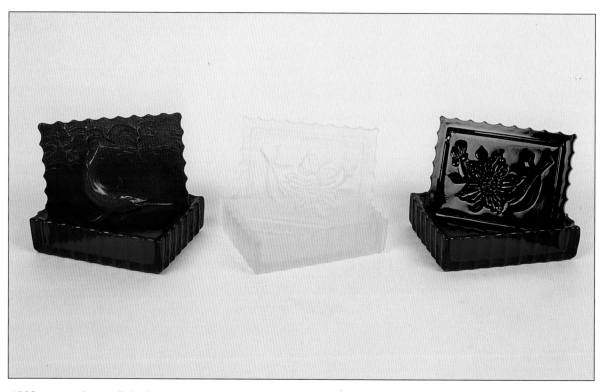

#308 cigarette boxes: Ruby bottom with bronze lid with sailfish, $150-175. Crystal Satin, $125-150. Ruby bottom with black lid, $125-150 (black bottom not known). *Courtesy of Dave & Linda Rash.*

Chapter 11
Noniridized Opalescent Colors

Amberina

#5 220 & 222 Amberina lemonade pitchers (only
a few known): #220, $500+; #222, $800+.

Amethyst

#950 Amethyst Opalescent cornucopias.
Very few sets known. $250+.

#950 Amethyst Opalescent console set.
Note different tops. $350+.

#6 11" Amethyst swan bowl. $150-175.
Courtesy of Fenton Museum.

Persian Pearl Stretch, $250+; #1681 Amethyst Big Cookies baskets, one known, $300+. *Courtesy of Dale & Eileen Robinson.*

Aquamarine

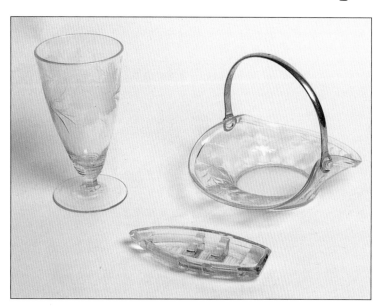

#1641-1702 Aquamarine Diamond Optic bridge goblet, $45-60.
Canoe ashtray (see Novelties for price).
#1614 Basket, $65-80. *Courtesy of Fenton Museum.*

#1502 Aquamarine cut candlestick, $75-95 pr.; #1536 6" compote with cutting, $100-125; #1533 dolphin compote, $65-75. *Courtesy of Fenton Museum.*

#1502A Aquamarine dolphin handled tray with cutting. $75-110.
Courtesy of Charles Griggs.

Blue

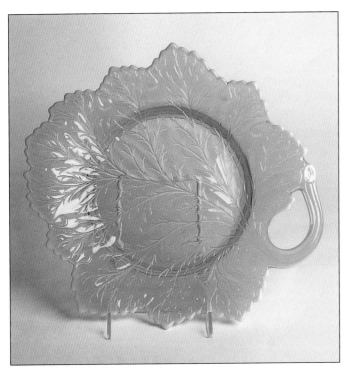

#175 Blue Opalescent 11" leaf cake plate, $100-125. *Courtesy of Ed & Pat Anderson.*

#1533 Blue Opalescent dolphin compote, $85-125. *Courtesy of Charles Griggs.*

Cameo

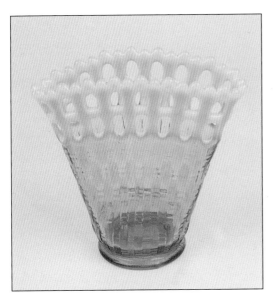

Oval handled server, $75-110. (This is the only one the author has seen.) *Courtesy of Bill Crowl.*

#1091 Cameo Opalescent swung fan vase. (Two known.) $100-150. *Courtesy of Bill Crowl.*

Covered jar Cameo Opalescent (shown on page 146 in *American Iridescent Stretch Glass* book – chapter on US Glass), $75-100; #1091 fan vase, $100-150; #923 Oval compote, $65-86. *Courtesy of Bill Crowl.*

#1608 10 1/2" dolphin footed bowl. (This is the first one this author has seen.) $275-325. *Courtesy of Bill Crowl.*

#923 Cameo Opalescent mayonnaise, $50-75. (Has anyone seen a ladle?)
#736 1 lb. candy, $75-100. *Courtesy of Ed & Pat Anderson.*

#1604 rolled 11" footed bowl, $275-325.

#1504 10" dolphin bowl, $85-115; #1533 6" compote, $65-85. *Courtesy of Ed & Pat Anderson.*

#1563 17" bowl. One known in Cameo Opalescent. $250-300. *Courtesy of Melvin & Norma Lampton.*

#1672 rolled edge candle, $75-100 pr.; #848 Petal bowl, $75-100. *Courtesy of Ed & Pat Anderson.*

Possible Fenton covered box, $65-90. (Looks to be the same shape as the US Glass example pictured on page 146 of *American Iridescent Stretch Glass*.) Coaster, $30-35; #3 sugar, $45-60. *Courtesy of Ed & Pat Anderson.*

#1635 10 oz. spiral optic tumbler, $35-45; unknown #, 7" tumbler. Possibly Fenton 5" spiral optic tumbler, $35-45. *Courtesy of Ed & Pat Anderson.*

#200 guest set, $350-425; tumble up, $100-130. *Courtesy of Ed & Pat Anderson.*

#621 6" vase, $75-85; #1512 9" flared bowl, $110-135. *Courtesy of Ed & Pat Anderson.*

#2 rib optic sugar, $125-150; #1636 jug, $225-275; #1636 iced tea, $45-65. *Courtesy of Fenton Museum.*

#1532 candy jar, $95-125;
#1533 fan vase, $55-65.

#3 Cameo Opalescent
creamer/sugar, $95-135 pr.

#950 Cameo Opalescent bowl. (This is the only one the author
has seen. Would anyone have the candles?) $150-175.

Possibly #184 12" Cameo
Opalescent vase. One
known. $150-175.

174

Celeste Blue

#53 Celeste Blue dresser set on #1502 tray. Powder, $95-125. Perfumes, $100-125 ea. Tray, $65-85. *Courtesy of Gordon & Sue Phifer.*

#220 covered lemonade pitcher and tumbler with unusual cutting. Pitcher, $350-400. Tumbler, $75-85. *Courtesy of Kevin Lavender.*

Green

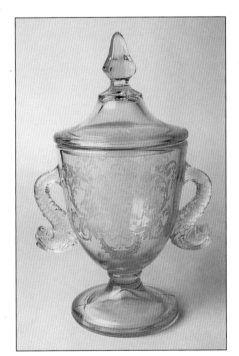

#1532 green dolphin candy jar, with unknown acid etching. (Looks similar to a New Martinsville etch, but not exact.) $85-125. *Courtesy of Charles Griggs.*

Detail of etching on the #1532 green dolphin candy jar.

Rose

#1608 Rose 10 1/2" oval bowl, $200-250. *Courtesy of John Walk.*

#1502 Rose 7 oz. bridge goblet, $25-30; ashtray without "F", Price Und.; #1636 iced tea, $35-45; #1636 pitcher, $200-250. *Courtesy of Fenton Museum.*

#1532 cut candy jar, $100-125.

Ruby

#1533 Ruby Opalescent flared compote. (Excellent example of what can happen with heat sensitive glass.) Price Und. *Courtesy of Charles Griggs.*

#1533 compote, Price Und.; #318 candlestick, Price Und.

#573 Ruby Opalescent rolled vase. Price Und.

Ruby #180 Hyacinth vase, one known, $175-200. #1700-1800 Lincoln Inn Sheffield match holder. Usually found in crystal, aquamarine, and amber. (This is the first Ruby the author has seen). $75-100. #1554 flowerpot. $95-125. *Courtesy of Dale & Eileen Robinson.*

#1502 Ruby Diamond Optic vanity set, $450-600.

Ruby two piece reamer, $800-1000. (These are rare.) Also known in Jade, black, Chinese Yellow, and Pekin Blue. Jade & black, $900-1200 ea.; Chinese Yellow & Pekin Blue, $2000 ea. *Courtesy of Fenton Museum.*

#184 6" Amber vase with cutting. $75-125; #184 12" Ruby with cutting, $150-175. Usually the 12" size can be found. Any 8", 6" or 4" vases are scarce.

#149 10" bowl. (Scarce shape.) $75-95.

Tangerine

#1502 Tangerine Diamond Optic dolphin compote, $100-150.

#918/1502 High standard compote. One known. $275-375. *Courtesy of Randy & Debbie Coe.*

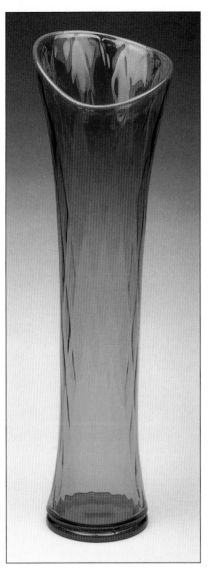

#573 8" rolled vase, $125-150. *Courtesy of Randy & Debbie Coe.*

#1502/1530 16" swung vase, $200-250. *Courtesy of Randy & Debbie Coe.*

Topaz

#1533 Topaz Opalescent dolphin fan vase, $125-150. *Courtesy of Nick Duncan.*

#2 Blue Opalescent Rib Optic creamer/sugar, $200-250 pr.

Spiral Optic 4" creamer with black handle (seen in Coin Spot & Green Opalescent), $125-175. *Courtesy of Thomas K. Smith.*

#222 Blue Opalescent vase (lemonade pitcher mold), $250-300.

#2 Green Opalescent satin rib optic creamer & sugar, $225-275.

#1590 4" coasters: Royal Blue, $20-30; Vaseline, $20-30; Chinese coral? (Fenton or Northwood?), $20-30; Jade, $30-35. *Courtesy of Gordon & Sue Phifer.*

#891 12" Green Opalescent Rib Optic vase. (This author is aware of fewer than five of these. One was sold four years ago for $425). $400-500.

Chapter 12
Satin Treatments

Ming

#920 Grape & Cable three part covered candy box. It is similar to the #1800 Silver Tone box. Price Und.

Detail of the Grape & Cable candy box.

#893 Green Ming ginger jar, lid and base, $200-275; #457 Green Ming stack set, two pieces of three with lid, $200-250 as shown.

#249 bowl, $95-110; #1684 macaroon jar with lid, $125-175. *Courtesy of Kill Creek Antiques.*

#1653 Rose Ming pitcher with black handle,
$150-200. Rare pitcher coaster, $75-100.

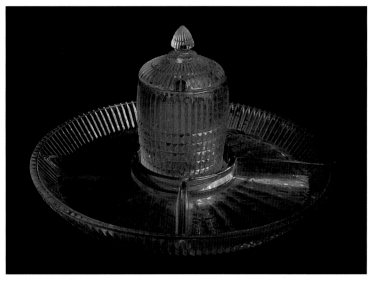

#893 Ming ginger jar in ormolu holder. $225-275.
Courtesy of Randy & Debbie Coe.

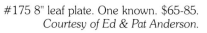

#175 8" leaf plate. One known. $65-85.
Courtesy of Ed & Pat Anderson.

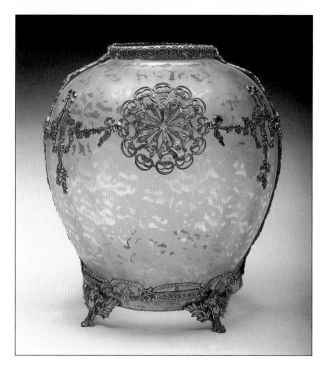

#1700-1800 Lincoln Inn Sheffield Ming relish, no lid, $125-
150 as shown. (Mr. Frank Fenton would like to find a lid for
this piece.) *Courtesy of Fenton Museum.*

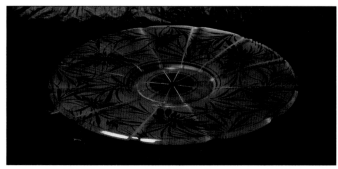

Mold unknown, 14" paneled torte plate with Poinsettia etching,
$85-115.

San Toy

#1260 two piece Ming baby reamer, $150-200; #5889 two piece Ming cigarette box & lid, $125-150; #844 flower finial bonbon in Wisteria, $175-225; #1590 San Toy coaster, $20-25; #705 San Toy ivy ball & base, $150-175. *Courtesy of Gordon & Sue Phifer.*

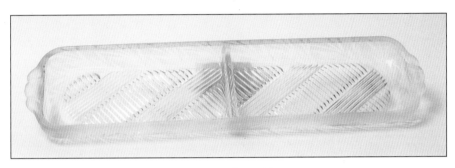

Mold unknown, 12" two part San Toy relish, $75-100.

#1934 San Toy decanter set on tray. Decanter, $150-175; whiskeys, $20-25 each; tray, $65-75. *Courtesy of Gordon & Sue Phifer.*

#893 San Toy ginger jar lamp, $150; #54 vanity tray, $75-100; #894 Poinsettia lamp, $100-150.

#184 Amber San Toy vase, $100-125; #180 Amber San Toy Hyacinth vase with Fenton label, $200-250. *Courtesy of Gordon & Sue Phifer.*

#180 Hyacinth San Toy vase. $125-150.

Detail of label on #180 Hyacinth vase. *Courtesy of Gordon & Sue Phifer.*

Scenic

#848 Petal bowl, $175-225; #1564 square planter, $225-250; #846 covered bonbon, $225-275. Scenic is second only to Twin Ivy as the most difficult to find. Scenic/Twin Ivy pieces are commanding premium prices when sold.

#846 covered bonbon, $225-275. *Courtesy of Gordon & Sue Phifer.*

#1934 5" triangle vase, $150-175. *Courtesy of Fenton Museum.*

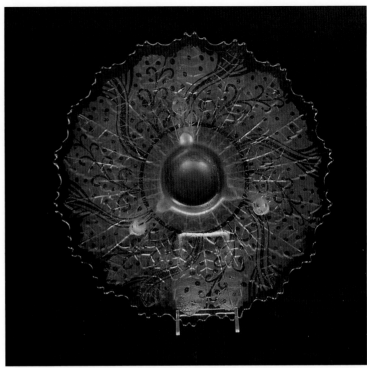

#1790 Leaf Tiers plate, Snow Fern, $175-225.
Courtesy of Gordon & Sue Phifer.

#249 6" Snow Fern* candlestick, $125-175 pair; #249 7 1/2"
Snow Fern* cupped bowl, $125-150.
(*Snow Fern is one of the rarest etchings. I have seen less than a
dozen pieces in fifteen years.)

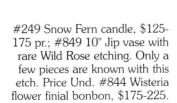

#249 Snow Fern candle, $125-
175 pr.; #849 10" Jip vase with
rare Wild Rose etching. Only a
few pieces are known with this
etch. Price Und. #844 Wisteria
flower finial bonbon, $175-225.

Twin Ivy

Twin Ivy etching is the most sough after etch. There are a few fortunate collectors who own more than one piece. Twin Ivy pieces are worth a minimum of $200 each. You be the judge of how much more you should pay if you locate a piece, realizing you may wait years before you see another piece.

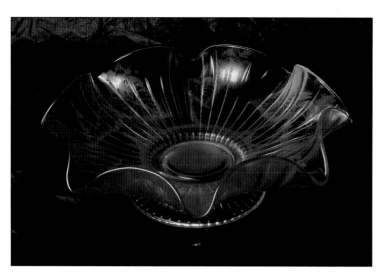

#231 11" bowl, $200+.

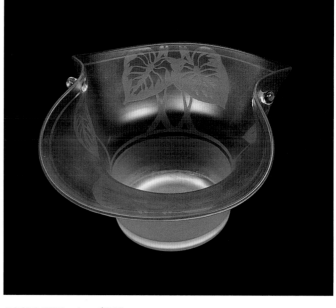

#1616 10" basket, $200+.

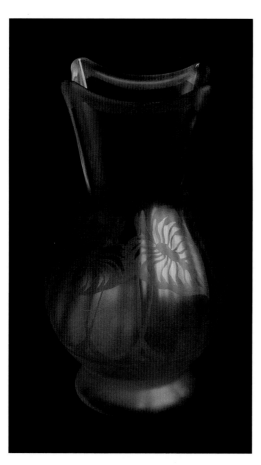

#894 10" Twin Ivy square top vase, $300+.

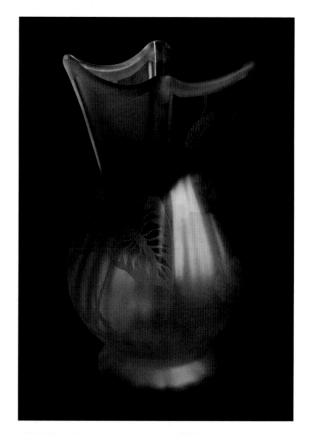

#894 Twin Ivy square top vase, $300+.
(Showing decoration on top.)

Viking

Rare Satin Viking bowl. This bowl and matching candlesticks are much sought after by collectors.
My advice is that if you find any of these pieces, you should buy them. Price Und.

Satin Viking Twin candlesticks. These
are rarer than the bowl. Price Und.

Wild Rose

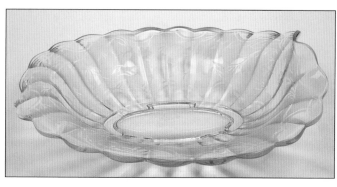

#1663 12" Wild Rose bowl. Price Und. *Courtesy of Thomas K. Smith.*

#1938 Wild Rose etching: very late etching. Only a few pieces are known. #170 two piece Hurricane with base. Price Und. #950 cornucopia bowl & #950 cornucopia candle. Prices Und. *Courtesy of Fenton Museum.*

Wild Rose 7" bowl. This is the only one the author has seen. $225+.

Wisteria

Rare eleven piece Wisteria punch set. This is only the second one that has turned up. Price Und.

Fourteen piece Wisteria flared punch set. This set has flared cups and the previous set cups are straight sided. $500-600. *Courtesy of Charles Griggs.*

#844 Wisteria flower finial candy, $175-225.

#200 Wisteria guest set. $200-275; #621 6" vase on base. Vase, $75-90. Base (ginger jar), $75-100. *Courtesy of Gordon & Sue Phifer.*

#33 Wisteria cocktail shaker, $100-125. Possibly a variation on the #200 guest set mold made into a decanter bottle. Only one known. Price Und.

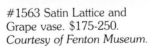

#1563 Satin Lattice and Grape vase. $175-250. *Courtesy of Fenton Museum.*

#349 8" Wisteria fan vase, $125-150; #184 8" vase, $75-100.

#1355 Wisteria pitcher & tumbler. Pitcher, $175-250; tumbler, $50-60.

Chapter 13
Lamps

B-10 Jade & Moonstone, B-20 Jade, $175+ each.

G70 Amber Satin with cutting, $275+; B10 Amber & Black,
$175+; G70 Blue Opalescent Rib Optic, $275+.

B-20 Celeste Blue & Moonstone, $200+ each.
Courtesy of Charles Griggs.

G-80 Topaz Opalescent Dot Optic & black bases, $175+ each.

#893 Jade ginger jar lamp with cutting, $375+.

G-70 Green Opalescent Pancake lamp, Rib Optic base & rare Drape Optic chimney, $400+.

Bibliography and Other Helpful Information

Coe, Debbie and Randy. *Elegant Glass*. Atglen, Pennsylvania: Schiffer Publishing, 2004.

Doty, David. *A Field Guide to Carnival Glass*. Marietta, Ohio: Antique Publications, 1998.

Edwards, Bill. *Standard Encyclopedia of Carnival Glass*. Paducah, Kentucky: Schroeder, 2000.

Heacock, William. *Fenton Glass, The First Twenty Five Years*. Marietta, Ohio: O-Val Advertising Corp., 1978.

Heacock, William. *Fenton Glass, The Second Twenty Five Years*. Marietta, Ohio: O-Val Advertising Corp., 1980.

Madeley, John and Dave Shetlar. *American Iridescent Stretch Glass*. Paducah, Kentucky: Schroder, 1998.

Mordini, Tom and Sharon. *Carnival Glass Auction Prices*. Freeport, Illinois: Mordini, Yearly Publication.

Umbraco, Kitty and Russell. *Iridescent Stretch Glass*. Berkeley, California: Ambura and Avery, 1972.

Whitmyer, Margarett and Kenn. *Fenton Art Glass, 1907-1939*. Paducah, Kentucky: Schroeder, 1996.

Wiggins, Berry. *Stretch in Color*. Orange, Virginia: Green, 1971.

Fenton Collectors Clubs

Fenton Art Glass Collectors of America
P.O. Box 384
Williamstown, WV 26187

National Fenton Glass Society
P.O. Box 4008
Marietta, OH 45750

Pacific Northwest Fenton Association
8225 Kilchis River Road
Tillamook, OR 97141

Carnival Glass Information

There are over twenty Carnival Glass clubs throughout the United States. Membership in one or more clubs is recommended for all serious collectors. Though I will not list them all here, there is a website that I highly recommended for all collectors. Visit: http://www.cga. All types of educational information are available along with auction calendars, links to the clubs, chat room, and other important information. When visiting the www.cga site, click on the link and visit: http://www.woodsland.com/carnivalglass